Advance praise for
Challenging the Law Enforcement Organization...

"Outstanding and overdue. Jack Enter's book, like his oral presentations, hit home in a big way because the truths he offers are both simple and insightful—and we cannot help but recognize ourselves captured by his discussions and examples."

Gary Deland
Director
Utah Sheriff's Association

"A superb piece of work! *Challenging the Law Enforcement Organization* is a vital blueprint for individual and social transformation and survival, as our society teeters on the brink in an ever more complex and dysfunctional world. This book must receive maximum distribution in the law enforcement community. It is a timeless resource that will save lives and change lives by transforming leaders, organizations, and institutional cultures, for many years to come.

"But the potential application of *Challenging the Law Enforcement Organization* goes beyond law enforcement. Just as the business world is constantly applying lessons from military management, I believe this book is the vector for the business world to inject lessons learned in the demanding, unforgiving world of law enforcement."

Lt. Col. Dave Grossman
Author of *On Combat* and *On Killing*
www.killology.com

"In his book *Challenging the Law Enforcement Organization*, Dr. Jack Enter provides a rare gift to leaders and aspiring leaders in the public safety profession. He draws on his unique combination of experiences as an applied law enforcement practitioner and leader, university professor, and nationally acclaimed public safety leadership trainer to create a readable, innovative, and insightful review of the challenges and responsibilities of leadership."

Kevin M. Gilmartin, Ph.D.
Author of *Emotional Survival for Law Enforcement*
Emotionalsurvival.com

"Every law enforcement manager will find himself throughout the pages of this book. For those of us who are still on our journey to joining the 10 percent who are truly effective leaders, Dr. Enter has provided provocative insights and an excellent road map for the trip."

Richard Crouch
Chief of Police
Gadsden Police Department, Alabama

"From start to finish, this book is an excellent resource for leaders at every level of experience. Whether you have been leading for thirty years or less than one year, you will benefit from the brilliant ideas and sound principles in this book. It is an essential reference for law enforcement managers who take seriously their most important responsibilities-becoming, and selecting, competent leaders of character for the twenty-first century."

Mark W. Field
Chief of Police
Wheaton Police Department, Illinois

"Several times a month, I get the opportunity to listen to another law enforcement guru who is preaching the topic de jour about how our profession is all screwed up and bad things are just going to happen. Jack is one of the rare exceptions to the standard doom and gloom preachers. When I first heard him speak (and most of you who have heard him will agree), I immediately started looking at my personal and professional life. The advice I learned from his short program worked for me. I know it will work for you and your law enforcement team.

"Simply stated, this book captures the heart and soul of Jack Enter's message. It is a brilliant synopsis of what is currently going on in the world and in our profession that impacts us personally and professionally. Thanks, Jack, for all you have done for our noble profession and for finally writing it all down."

Gordon Graham
Graham Research Consultants

Challenging *the* Law Enforcement Organization

CHALLENGING *the* LAW ENFORCEMENT ORGANIZATION

Proactive Leadership Strategies

Jack E. Enter, Ph.D.

NARROW ROAD PRESS

Printed in the United States of America.

1 2 3 4 5 6 7 8 9 10—03 02 01 00

First printing, June 2006

ISBN: 0-9785537-0-5

Published by
Narrow Road Press
P.O. Box 2238
Dacula, GA 30019-9998
www.jackenter.com

Library of Congress Control Number: 2006927389

Dedication

This book is dedicated first to my wife, Barbara; my sons, Jason and Travis; and my daughter, Rebekah. Their sacrifices and patience with me throughout these many years have allowed much of what is contained in this book to come to fruition. They are my foremost leadership responsibility, and I am thankful for the mercy and forgiveness they have shown me through the ups and downs of my roles as a father and a husband. My wife has demonstrated many of the skills detailed in this book and has been a role model of what it is like to be a leader—to stand before an audience of One.

The book is also dedicated to the thousands of law enforcement professionals—past, present, and future—who have chosen or will choose the wonderful career of guardian in our remarkable country. May this book be a small form of assistance in helping them to better serve the public, their fellow professionals, and their families.

The ultimate dedication must be reserved, however, to the One who has had the most influence on my personal life and on most of the principles in this book. Any success that I have enjoyed in my personal and professional life has been because of my Lord's mercy and grace. The upcoming discussion of the critical skills of discipline, servanthood, humility, encouragement, and accountability are clear throughout the Bible, and we would be most presumptuous to assume that leadership is a new and modern concept. Christ not only walked the narrow road, He invented it, and His influence as a leader will continue to be felt throughout the world—and in the world to come.

Contents

Acknowledgments

I would like to express my appreciation to the following individuals, whose support and guidance made this book possible. Though I have thought about writing a book for years, Kevin Gilmartin, Dave Grossman, and Mark Field encouraged me to put these intentions on paper—and for that I will always be in their debt. Much of the intellectual content in these chapters comes from several sources. Steve Sampson's mentoring on the importance of social skills is stamped throughout much of this book; he has taught me more than any other person about life skills and human behavior. I am also thankful to the law enforcement managers who shared their experiences and successes with me. Their stories not only substantiate the problems we face in law enforcement but also offer real solutions. Finally, I have had the privilege to know personally leaders who managed to walk the narrow road both at work and at home. They have shown me that it is possible to be a leader in a world that is starving for leadership.

Foreword

Eight years ago, I tried diligently to change the organizational culture of my police agency. Two years ago, my church of about one thousand tried to reinvent itself within our men's ministry to develop and mentor future leaders. Jack Enter was there to guide us through both efforts.

Jack was a critical person, at a critical time, who brought about organizational transformation within our men's ministry and police department. I still hear members of the Wheaton Police Department command staff use Jack's quotes and quips, and we continue to use his principles weekly. His emphasis on day-to-day reality rather than abstract leadership theory revitalized my own leadership, and I constantly hear Jack's precepts ringing in my ear: "You must invade their culture . . . get out of your office . . . you must invade their culture. You know who you are—you haven't set foot in a squad car, worn a uniform, or been on the street for years."

If leading people in your organization is among your most critical responsibilities, then you need to read this book. *Challenging the Law Enforcement Organization* offers invaluable leadership insight and draws from the author's professional law enforcement and military leadership experiences, knowledge, and worldwide lectures. What distinguishes it from other leadership books is Jack's candid presentation of the most common leadership mistakes and realistic and practical approaches for the reader to overcome them. For example, the action items not only help strengthen readers' understanding of the concepts, they push readers into immediately acting on those concepts. Many lecturers communicate without anyone really learning anything, pushing content without applying that content to real life or using creativity to ensure learning. Jack's lectures and this book are clearly set apart from that approach.

The transparency and vulnerability that he practices before a live audience are truly reflected in this book, which is skillfully crafted with a two-fold goal in mind: to help law enforcement leaders improve their personal leadership toolkit and to help them take their organizations from good to great. Every leader at every level needs to read this book— police officers, detectives, sergeants, lieutenants, directors, superintendents, chiefs, commissioners—whatever kind of group or organization you lead. It can revolutionize your leadership.

—Mark W. Field
Chief of Police
Wheaton Police Department, Illinois

Introduction

Numerous issues make the roles of police supervisors and managers more challenging than they have been at perhaps any other time. As chapter 1 illuminates in a discussion of external influences on a law enforcement agency, American society is a socially unskilled culture engaged in *fight or flight* behaviors, marked by

> *Do not go where the path may lead, go instead where there is no path and leave a trail.*
> —**Ralph Waldo Emerson**

aggression, frustration, addiction, and violence. Police applicants who can pass a polygraph, drug test, and background investigation seem increasingly harder to find. Allegations of racial profiling and brutality as well as other external criticisms regularly appear in the media. Few would say that any of this will change for the better in the immediate future.

How are American law enforcement managers rising to meet these challenges? Chapter 2 explores the internal influences on a law enforcement agency. At a recent law enforcement conference, a researcher summarized his findings indicating that ineffective supervisors and managers may be one of the strongest sources of stress for law enforcement personnel. This conclusion is supported by literally thousands of interviews I have conducted. When I asked personnel whether they ever wanted to quit the profession, most responded affirmatively. When I asked why, they consistently answered along the lines of, "There was this guy who was my lieutenant. . . ." One police chief remarked that the number one problem facing the law enforcement profession was that "we are overmanaged and underled." I could not agree more.

Only a small percentage of law enforcement managers are perceived as consistently demonstrating leadership in the organizational culture. Conversely, most managers are perceived as inconsistent, reactive communicators who show favoritism in their dealings with subordinates. Law enforcement agencies send these managers to leadership training programs, yet when these individuals return to the agency, they show no positive change in their behavior or leadership strategies. Line personnel complain about their sergeants, and then these same line personnel are promoted and exhibit the same behaviors as those sergeants. What causes the majority of law enforcement managers to fail to practice leadership consistently in the organizational culture? Better yet is the question, what factors cause the small percentage of effective managers to practice leadership consistently and to affect their agencies positively?

> *It is interesting that in a profession often requiring one to engage violent offenders and deal with dangerous situations, personnel seem more frustrated with and afraid of fellow personnel.*

Chapters 3 and 4 attempt to answer these questions with explanations and examples of effective and ineffective leadership. Chapters 5 through 8 explore in more depth the characteristics of those "abnormal" law enforcement managers who seem to practice leadership consistently in their careers. Chapter 5 focuses on leaders' perceptions of themselves and their roles as managers and how they achieve a sort of self-mastery so that they lead by example. Chapter 6 describes their ability to communicate proactively and engage those around them and to break down the resistance and mistrust of some of the most negative and suspicious human beings on earth. Chapter 7 illuminates how effective managers reinforce their leadership by encouraging good behavior and by confronting marginal and problem behavior. Chapter 8 reveals how you can apply leadership skills to your personal life and why doing this is critical to your professional success.

Since I began my law enforcement career in 1972, I have seen many changes in technology, liability, and the nature of violent crime. As a member of the first generation of college-educated police officers, I, like the others, felt we would be different from and better than our predecessors.

In some ways we were, but we did not see much success in leadership. It is time, as we spend our twilight years in this wonderful profession, to make a change in the way we approach leadership. We owe it to the public, to our profession, and to our younger colleagues as they prepare to take the mantle from us. Those who are just getting started in their careers likewise owe it to themselves and their peers to accept that mantle and take the profession to a level beyond what my generation thought possible.

External Influences on Law Enforcement Culture

Many factors in American society and culture influence law enforcement organizations. External factors, such as operational and crime issues, internally influence the law enforcement agency in recruitment and other personnel areas. Later chapters in this book demonstrate how the skills-related issues examined in this chapter are critical to understanding leadership success and failure. Before taking a hard look at American culture, however, I want to emphasize that criticizing American society does not mean I feel we live in a terrible society; I believe we live in the greatest country in the world. We must, however, look with a critical eye at what is happening in American culture if we are to understand crime today and in the next decades.

Violence and Skills

Why does the United States, despite its incredible wealth and technology, have significant levels of violent predatory crime, mental health issues, addiction, and other social problems? If poverty is the reason, then why are many of these social problems also found among the wealthiest segments of our society? If violent crime is due to the presence of too many firearms, then why don't other countries (like Switzerland, whose male population in the military reserves keep automatic weapons in their homes) have the same problem? Though the causes of crime are complex, I believe we can at least begin to understand American crime and social problems from the perspective of skills. How do human beings become socialized so that they have the required skills to live in a culture without resorting to violence and addictions or succumbing to mental health problems?

What skills make us successful at work and in relationships?
How would you describe a person you know who is successful, or skilled, at life? I am not talking about just financial success but success in all aspects of life. All who know the person agree that he or she is a great person to be around. When I ask this question in seminars, participants often list the following characteristics, or skills:

> honesty and integrity
> unselfishness
> dependability
> self-discipline
> communication skills
> work ethic
> kindness

Whatever list you may come up with, skills of successful people normally fall into two areas:

> **Intrapersonal skills** (the ability to manage oneself)—self-discipline, honesty and integrity, self-awareness, and so on.
>
> **Interpersonal skills** (the ability to deal with other people)—oral communication, nonverbal communication, listening, and so on.

Most people agree that these two categories of skills are critical to success in any society. Though technical skills are also important, if people do not have the basic ability to manage their own behavior and the skills to interact with other human beings, they are going to have a difficult time in our society or in any other. Ted Kaczynski, the Unabomber, is an excellent example of this point. Though he had significant intellectual skills, far greater than those of most Americans, he was hugely deficient in his intrapersonal and interpersonal skills; these deficiencies overwhelmed his substantial educational and intellectual achievements.

Where and how do human beings learn intrapersonal and interpersonal skills?
If one of society's major responsibilities is to socialize human beings, what tools are usually used to accomplish this important undertaking? The list you and others come up with will often have these social institutions listed:

- family and extended family
- neighborhood and community
- school
- church, temple, or other place of worship
- peers

How well are social institutions fulfilling their role in American culture?
How effectively do these institutions take infants and train them throughout life to be skilled in the most complex society on the face of the earth? I warn those who are strongly politically correct that they may not enjoy the next section of this discussion.

Family and extended family. Though there are many wonderful, effective families and extended families in the United States, I propose that they are not the norm by any stretch of the imagination. If you have worked in law enforcement, education, or social services, you will likely agree that there is limited socialization and adult modeling

Parents generally love their children, but many do not attend to their children's instruction, discipline, or skill development.

among U.S. families. Parents generally love their children, but many do not attend to their children's instruction, discipline, or skill development. Even in two-parent families, both mother and father have increasingly become involved in their own careers (which often exceed the stereotypical forty hours a week), and they are emotionally exhausted when they get home. These parents will buy their children what they want, sign them up for karate classes and soccer, but will generally not take the time to *engage* (spend time, communicate, and become involved with) or to make sure these children are learning the necessary skills to excel in this culture. Disciplining and training children to control their anger, exercise self-control, and master other critical skills have been replaced with a focus on entertainment and material bribery, not on accountability.

Disciplining and training children to control their anger, exercise self-control, and master other critical skills have been replaced with a focus on entertainment and material bribery, not on accountability.

In most cultures, the extended family (grandparents, aunts, uncles, and so on) has played an important role in socializing children. This traditional social backup system for parents in our culture and in most cultures in other countries has been in transition in recent decades. In today's tremendously transient society, the extended family doesn't live down the street or even in the same city. Family members often live too far from each other to provide adult modeling for all the children in their family. Thus, the role of family and extended family in today's culture is often minimal. A psychologist friend of mine calls the American culture an "unattended to" society, which unfortunately is an appropriate description for the effects traditional social institutions such as family have on modern American culture.

Other social institutions. Do other institutions, such as neighborhoods and schools, do a better job of teaching interpersonal and intrapersonal skills? Experiences in community policing and crime prevention programs often reveal that many Americans do not know the names of *any* of their neighbors. Neighbors are strangers, far from playing a part in adult modeling and accountability. (Conversely, how many of you boomers were snitched out to your parents by the lady down the street?) Schools also generally take a hands-off approach to dealing with their students. Who can blame them? Parents are not likely to support a school's discipline or accountability measures. In previous generations, a telephone call from a teacher or principal usually resulted in parents disciplining their children and supporting the school in the educational and instructional process. Now, any disciplinary action a school takes against a child is likely to produce threats of litigation.

Peers. Peers are often regarded as purely negative influences, but they can have a positive role in the socialization process. In peer relationships, we learn how to get along with others. When we played with other children in our neighborhoods, what skills did we learn? We learned not to be selfish, how to work within a group, how to lose, and other skills that would eventually serve us well in the workplace. Peers can be a primary learning vehicle for intrapersonal and interpersonal skills. If you were rude and selfish as a child in traditional society, you were either disciplined or ostracized by the group —serious consequences when neighborhood play was the primary form of entertainment. Are peers still a major institution of learning social skills? How often do you see children playing as you drive through a neighborhood? Probably not often—the kids are inside watching television or playing video games. The media are now the primary socialization tools in American culture. Though many of us are concerned about what these kids are watching, the most important concern should be that they are watching alone. They are participating in an artificial environment rather than learning social skills critical for a successful and emotionally fulfilling life.

Though many of us are concerned about what these kids are watching, the most important concern should be that they are watching alone.

What is the result of having no socialization skills?
From an *individualistic* perspective, this lack of skills development leads to many human beings having difficulty being socially and intrapersonally successful in our culture. From a *societal* perspective, the implications of not socializing our young men and women are dire. For people without the prerequisite skills to be successful in a complex culture, life can be emotionally stressful, frustrating, and bewildering.

Encouraging Poor Social Skills

Many people have had an experience similar to one I had in an airport, while sitting near my gate. A teenager sat across from me, listening to his personal stereo. His mother (I assume) tapped him on the shoulder, at which point he ripped off his stereo headset and yelled at her, "What the f . . . k do you want?" Obviously flustered, she responded, "I just wanted to know if you wanted something to eat before we got on the plane." He pointed his finger at her, said, "Why don't you leave me the f . . . k alone," and replaced his headset. Her response to this was interesting; she genuinely and contritely responded, "I am so sorry I bothered you." How well will this young man do in our culture, especially in the area of social and work relationships? I don't think his mother has done him any favors. He will have a difficult time being successful in relationships and in the work environment.

If you have ever been in a work or social environment without the skills or experience to successfully handle the situation, you know how stressful it can be. A police officer who does not speak Spanish being assigned to a patrol area where most of the citizens are Hispanic might have a difficult and frustrating experience. In the same way, Americans who do not have the skills to succeed in life find that they can't "speak the language" of the complex world around them. What is the normal reaction to frustration? If you have ever been asked to complete a task or job for which you have not been trained or in which you still do not feel proficient, what was your reaction? You became stressed, you perspired, your heart rate increased, and you became nervous. Why? Because your body sensed fear and uncertainty. The two commonly recognized psychological reactions to fear are *fight* and *flight*. Consider this individual response from a societal standpoint: complex emotional creatures who are not socially skilled will likely react to their fear by fight or flight. The prevalence of this reaction in our culture is integral to one of the most logical explanations for crime in American society. How?

> *People pay for what they do, and still more for what they have allowed themselves to become. And they pay for it very simply; by the lives they lead.*
>
> —James Baldwin

Fight Behavior

People who do not know how to handle the complex social demands of living in an industrialized society may *fight* by becoming aggressive toward individuals around them. American culture is unfortunately known for its aggression. We are likely the most predatory, violent society in the world. Though many countries suffer terrible violence, most of it is political or ideological, usually occurring in a group context, like the situations in Israel or Sudan. In America, however, violence is usually individual and either predatory (such as robbery and rape) or spontaneous (such as road rage and sports violence) because of anger and frustration. These two American typologies of violence and aggression

Socially unskilled

Fear and frustration

Fight   or   flight

are rare in most societies, especially the spontaneous typology, known as violence due to a lack of "frustrability"—the ability to handle frustration.

Frustrability is not a real word but a term coined to describe what individuals lack when they are unable to handle things not going their way. I believe that Americans experience spontaneous violence because many individuals in our society are unable to handle relational and work or school problems or to respond to people who "get in their way." In most societies and in previous American generations, parents and other adults taught children that life's events were not always going to work out; life was not always fair. When we educate our children to handle frustration, we tell them "no" when appropriate and enforce or explain consequences for wrongdoing, teaching them to conform to standards and learn to roll with the punches of life. Later in their lives, when events do not go as expected, they are able to handle frustration and disappointment.

> *I believe that Americans experience spontaneous violence because many individuals in our society are unable to handle relational and work or school problems or to respond to people who "get in their way."*

In today's society, many children and young adults do not have frustrability—they can't handle "no" because their parents have not allowed them to fail or to pay consequences. When these children don't obey, they are not punished but are given their privileges anyway. If they are failing in school or do not make the football team, it is not their fault—others were "unfair." Parents may even threaten the school or athletic association with a civil suit. Many parents try to overprotect their children from failure and disappointment. Later in life, however, these young people will find that others, and life in general, are not so accommodating. How does this relate to violence in America?

I am convinced that much of our violence is due to the lack of frustrability in many of our citizens. Aggressive driving (road rage), workplace violence, stalking, school shootings, and other random, seemingly senseless acts of violence are perpetrated by people who just can't handle criticism, rejection, sarcasm, and so forth. Most boomers I know were made fun of, dumped, or lost a job while in school. Why didn't we shoot people? Because our parents and most adults in society consistently told us "no" and that "life is not always fair," and they made us pay consequences when we were wrong. When we failed to get what we wanted or failed at something, it was just the latest series of disappointments we were not pleased with but were able to handle. I do not mean to idealize the upbringing of the boomers and other previous generations—we all had problems. I believe, however, that frustrability violence is and will continue to be much more prevalent in American culture than it was in the past. Much of our crime will be committed by individuals who are unskilled in coping with life and its complex and often disappointing forms.

Frustrability and School Violence

Many case studies of students who resort to violence against others attribute the violence to the perpetrator being previously harassed and picked on by other students. Though unkind behavior should never be condoned, I think we tend to forget that most of us were picked on in school but didn't commit violence against others. When I ask a class of law enforcement personnel how many were the subject of ridicule and jokes in high school, most raise their hands. The point is that the cruelty of high school students has always been with us. The difference is that some individuals in today's schools are so frustrated and unskilled in handling conflict and criticism that they resort to violence.

Flight Behavior

Not everyone who is unskilled intrapersonally and interpersonally will respond with violence and aggression. Many, if not most, individuals will opt to flee the bewildering society around them. How do Americans flee?

Substance abuse and addiction

Many people choose to flee everyday life by abusing alcohol or drugs. Chemical escape has permeated all American classes and cultures. Our society's population has significant substance abuse problems, and the nation's prisons and jails are filled with these individuals. Many social problems such as domestic violence and child abuse are often related to substance abuse. Can you imagine what American society would be like without drug and alcohol abuse?

Substance Abuse and Violent Crime

Some of my most educational experiences have been my exposures to inmates in correctional institutions who were incarcerated for violent crimes. What was striking to observe was that most of them seemed pretty normal in a controlled setting like a prison or jail; I was often surprised to find out someone was serving a sentence for a very violent crime. Many admitted that outside the correctional setting, they would abuse alcohol and drugs, which would often result in violent behavior they could control somewhat when sober or not on drugs. Many of the trustee inmates who work unsupervised as janitors in police departments are often serving time for homicide, usually as a result of a drunken rage against a spouse or acquaintance.

Other addictions

Not only do Americans abuse alcohol and drugs, they also become addicted to other forms of flight, or escape behavior. Some forms of escapism include compulsive gambling, sexual promiscuity, and watching pornography. Individuals who do not participate in the serious forms of addictive behaviors often engage in escape activities that are more socially acceptable. They may escape by watching too much television, spending many hours on the Internet, buying more than they can afford (addictive consumerism), and other activities that can be just as addictive as cocaine or alcohol. Most Americans are also overweight, and obesity may become the number one health problem of this century.

Overweight America

As a person who has been overweight much of his adult life, I find it amazing to go overseas and find that in most countries, being overweight is highly unusual. In most industrialized countries, only a small percentage of individuals are overweight, and even they are not generally as obese as the American public. I asked the Polish police when they came to the United States how Americans were different, and they enthusiastically responded that they were shocked at how fat Americans were. One Polish police commander noted that a popular television show in Poland was *Baywatch,* but he had noticed that very few people in America looked like the actors on that program. Another individual, from South Africa, was amazed at the food portions served in American eating establishments—literally two or three times the amounts served in most countries.

Emotional and mental health problems

We should not be surprised that without nurturing, discipline, and healthy relationships, complex emotional creatures like us will have emotional and mental health problems. Living in a culture without the prerequisite skills places significant stress on a person's emotional state. The most prescribed medications in the United States are not for physical ailments, but for emotional and mental ones. Our prisons and jails have unwittingly become mental health institutions, with significant percentages of the inmates needing psychological and psychiatric intervention.

American law enforcement has increasingly been forced to deal with mentally disturbed individuals in society. Much of the development of less-than-lethal force (such as rubber bullets and stun guns) is attributed to the increased number of encounters with the emotionally disturbed. Being frustrated and unskilled in American culture has had serious psychological implications in our society.

Living in a Complex and Changing Society

Policing a society of individuals who do not have adequate social and emotional skills is further complicated by the significant and exponential change occurring in American culture. Intra- and interpersonal skills are important in all societies but are especially critical in societies undergoing transition and flux. Change necessitates adaptability, an intrapersonal attribute usually found only in the more skilled and mature individuals of a culture. In a society that has failed to socialize many of its inhabitants, change can aggravate social and crime issues. The following trends are some of those that will transform American society and criminal justice.

In a society that has failed to socialize many of its inhabitants, change can aggravate social and crime issues.

The demographic diversification of American culture

Fight or flight reactions demonstrate the influence of fear on behavior. One common type of fear is a *phobia*, such as *claustrophobia*, fear of close spaces, or *acrophobia*, fear of heights. One of the most common phobias in human behavior, likely present in everyone, is *xenophobia*—the fear of people who are different. This common fear of different cultures and people is important to this discussion because the United States is undergoing significant demographic change. After centuries of a culture dominated primarily by white Europeans and African Americans, the United States is receiving new immigrants from myriad different cultures. Hispanics and Latinos have dominated this new wave of American residents, now outnumbering African Americans as the largest minority group in the country. Add Asians and Pacific Islanders, Arabs, Russians, and other nontraditional groups to the mix and one can see that America may be undergoing one of its most complex demographic transitions in history. The continued influence of ethnic gangs, new organized crime groups, domestic and international terrorism, and claims of racial profiling will add a complicated multicultural dimension to American crime and law enforcement operational demands.

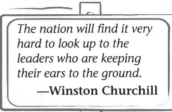

The nation will find it very hard to look up to the leaders who are keeping their ears to the ground.

—Winston Churchill

Xenophobia and September 11

Most of us remember what we were doing the morning of September 11, 2001. I was alone at my home in Atlanta, typing on my computer, without any television or radio playing, oblivious to what was going on. That situation was rectified when I answered the door for a carpet installer who had an appointment to repair our carpet. He immediately blurted out that someone had flown a plane into the World Trade Center. He followed me to my den, where I turned on my television, and we watched the drama of that day continue to unfold. When he learned that another plane had hit the trade center, he angrily blurted out, "We should never have let Hispanics into this country!"

I was flabbergasted that he was somehow connecting this to illegal immigration from Central and South America. When I asked him why he thought that, he thought for a second and told me that Hispanics had nothing to do with this attack. It occurred to me that when his views of American life had been threatened, he had immediately blamed the group that he had seen recently move into the Atlanta area for the first time. His angry response to the attacks of September 11 was a classic case of xenophobic behavior.

Economic uncertainty

Economic factors will always aggravate racial and ethnic differences. When societies undergo difficult economic times, individuals may respond to financial stressors by blaming certain groups for these problems or wanting to restrict future immigration. Hate crimes, the polarization of politics along racial lines, and other factors related to the economy will influence crime and such operational demands as policing mass demonstrations and union strikes. The most serious economic impact on American policing, however, is the impact on funding agency budgets. Many state and local law enforcement agencies are feeling the economic pressure of budget cuts and even personnel layoffs. After years of positive economic growth, most agencies are being asked to cut back programs and personnel at a time when crime is becoming more complex and demanding. The law enforcement agencies least affected by this recent economic downturn have been those federal agencies who have received substantial funding in response to homeland defense issues. Regardless of this exception, if the economic downturn continues or worsens, agency funding will have a strong influence on the operational and personnel strategies of America's law enforcement agencies.

After years of positive economic growth, most agencies are being asked to cut back programs and personnel at a time when crime is becoming more complex and demanding.

Other factors

In addition to demographic and economic challenges, American crime and U.S. law enforcement agencies are also influenced by such factors as technological advances and legal issues. The rapid growth of technology in the United States has brought many positive advances to American culture, but it has also brought new crimes, such as computer hacking, identity theft, and other economic crimes. Computer technology has also allowed child molesters, racist groups, and terrorists to spread destructive philosophies and facilitate

illicit operations. This easily accessible dissemination of extremist and destructive belief systems is compounded by the problem that parental supervision and instruction is likely at an all-time low.

At the same time, American culture has become more litigious and more prone to use the court system against a criminal justice agency. Many law enforcement agencies are continually responding to civil litigation by criminals, citizens, and even their own employees. Though some of these cases are obviously substantiated and necessary, many are not. Many law enforcement managers have become overly sensitive about being sued, which often translates into an increased emphasis on not being aggressive in operational matters or proactive on personnel issues.

The causes of crime in American culture, and the current and future social trends that affect crime, all influence the law enforcement mission. Is there hope that some of these issues will diminish if American society wakes up and begins

to respond to these problems? Yes, of course, but if we immediately rectified all the problems discussed in this chapter,
how long would it take to "undo" the impact of these problems? It took American society a decade or two to arrive at
its current state of problems and weaknesses. Many crimi-
nologists and sociologists believe that if we made an immediate all-out effort to rectify the problems we have created,
it would take *at least* ten to fifteen years to see the impact of
this reformation. The point is this: tremendous demands will
continue to be made on America's policing agencies to
respond to the country's significant social, economic, and
legal problems. If a law enforcement organization is to be
more effective in responding to these demands, it must have
effective leaders. The next two chapters examine the internal organizational culture and current management behaviors of today's organizations to determine if law enforcement
is able to rise to this challenge.

Internal Influences on Law Enforcement Culture

2

The Law Enforcement Perspective

Diversity

Unions and Employee Groups

Bad and Ineffective Managers

Each law enforcement agency has its own personality, but some factors seem common to most, if not all, policing institutions. Though many of these issues are also present in other professions, some are intensified in or restricted to those organizations tasked with policing American culture. Many issues endemic in the police culture will influence a leader's attempt to affect the organizational culture positively.

The Law Enforcement Perspective

One of the issues that strongly influences law enforcement officers and their organizations is their overall cynicism about human behavior. Cops are exposed to the worst that human behavior can produce. Repeated exposures to such crimes as child molestation, domestic violence, sexual assault, and homicide tend to make most police officers pessimistic about human behavior. Though individuals who commit these crimes and their victims represent only a small percentage of all people who live in the United States, law enforcement personnel are overexposed to this type of behavior and thus may naturally begin to view all humans as untrustworthy and prone to illegal or inappropriate behavior. This viewpoint can produce cynicism, alienation from the public, and a host of other problems. From a leadership perspective, how will this negative view of human behavior affect the management dimensions of the workplace? Let's examine a few of these dimensions.

First, cops tend not to trust a leader's motives or strategies to affect the culture positively. They will likely assume an agenda, or ulterior motive, when you attempt to implement the strategies in this book. If you try to spend time with them during their operational duties (management by walking around), they might immediately assume you are spying on them. Programs to reward exemplary behavior will probably be dismissed as touchy feely psychobabble or a way to reward the administrator's favorites. Those who wish to lead must remember that cops (like most people) don't want to hear promises—they want to see these promises put into action. Given the level of officer cynicism, leaders must not only put words into action but also follow through in the midst of often extended resistance and criticism. Winning over the law enforcement culture is not for the faint-hearted or the impatient.

> *Those who wish to lead must remember that cops (like most people) don't want to hear promises—they want to see these promises put into action.*

Another manner in which the law enforcement perspective affects the law enforcement culture is in how supervisors and managers view positive behavior by their subordinates. Cops have been operationally conditioned to notice bad or unwanted behavior. They tend to ignore good drivers and other well-behaved individuals; however, if someone starts driving foolishly or acting strangely, cop mental radar immediately locks in. This occupational focus on bad behavior ultimately affects supervisors and managers in two ways. First, they tend to *ignore good and exemplary behavior* in their subordinates. It does not get their attention. If an employee does an outstanding job, a supervisor might not reward the behavior or might even find something to criticize. Second, supervisors tend to *focus on disciplining* employees, because that is what they were operationally trained to do. Employee actions that are incorrect immediately get the attention and energy of supervisors who spent their operational career focused on catching bad guys. This overemphasis on reacting to mistakes while ignoring good and exemplary behavior is contrary to effective leadership strategies. I have heard of many instances of personnel who risk their lives to save others only to be verbally assaulted by supervisors, such as for not wearing their hat when rushing into a burning building to rescue someone. This reactive and overwhelmingly negative philosophy of managing others will always be at odds with attempts to implement leadership in a culture.

Finding Things Wrong

While teaching a class for a state police agency, I mentioned that supervisors often find something wrong with even commendable actions by their employees. A state trooper in the class then described a time when he was behind a motorist caught in traffic who went into cardiac arrest. The trooper called for an ambulance, pulled the citizen from the car, and began to administer CPR. As he was desperately trying to save the man's life through mouth-to-mouth resuscitation, he noticed from his kneeling position that among the feet of bystanders were the uniform shoes and pants of another state police officer. He then heard above him the loud voice of his supervisor asking him, "Where the hell is your hat?" Regulations required officers to always wear their hats when outside their vehicles. The supervisor was obviously concentrating on this minor administrative infraction rather than on the heroic efforts to save a life. Sadly, I have heard many variations of this story about two dozen times from law enforcement officers around the country.

The perspectives of younger employees

The philosophies and beliefs of the Generation X and Y employees also influence law enforcement culture. As chapter 1 describes, many young law enforcement personnel were raised in the "unattended to" American culture, with limited adult modeling or in a family and educational environment where authority and discipline were not emphasized. Though many of these young men and women are superb individuals, they often have drastically different perspectives than their older peers and managers. Though younger employees often possess higher levels of education and superior technical and computer skills compared with many older employees, these older employees and managers often resent the younger employees' attitudes and beliefs systems. Some of the most frequently mentioned attitudes and philosophies at odds with the older generation include

- self-centeredness—"me" perspective
- lack of career mindedness—minimal or no loyalty to an agency and the profession
- impatience regarding promotion and assignments—resistance to paying dues
- lack of respect for rank or seniority

Who Needs Experience?

When I was teaching at a university, one of my former students, now a police officer, came to my office for a visit. He told me that he had heard I might be going back to a command-level position in my former agency. When I informed him that I was considering the position, he asked, "Would you like to take me with you as a captain?" I reminded him that a captain in the agency was responsible for many employees, mostly experienced law enforcement personnel. I asked him how much experience he had in law enforcement, and he cheerfully replied, "Over six months!" I asked him did he think that qualified him to be a captain in an agency, and he confidently replied, "Absolutely!" Though I know it was probably unkind, I burst out laughing.

How do these attitudes influence a manager's ability to affect the culture? From a negative standpoint, these individualistic perspectives, if not recognized and responded to, can be an impediment to building team and agency cohesiveness. I have observed, however, that if young employees are sufficiently challenged, and the missions and goals are clearly defined, good leadership will bring them into the culture. The dedication and professionalism of our young men and women in the armed forces is an example of how this generation can be won over with proper leadership. Another positive characteristic of the younger generation is that they tend to be more candid and open about expressing their opinions and views than their older counterparts are. This openness, though sometimes uncomfortable to hear, can benefit the manager in analyzing the issues and problems within the agency.

The perspectives of older employees
Though many of law enforcement's older personnel and managers bring their experience and work ethic to the organizational culture, winning over the veterans offers managers different challenges than those associated with the younger employees. The younger generation is often criticized for its individualism and self-centeredness; older employees are most often noted for their cynicism and resistance to change. Although law enforcement personnel tend to be more cynical than most people, this cynicism is more dramatic among the older members of an agency and, in my experience, is usually focused on the agency itself.

Why do many older employees feel this animosity? Much of this cynicism is likely due to resentment. They feel that the agency has not repaid their years of service and personal sacrifice. As employees move through the second half of their careers, many cannot help noticing that their individual careers have been a disappointment; they did not achieve the promotions and assignments they had hoped for. Every supervisor and manager who is younger than they are is a constant reminder that their career goals were not realized. Combine this feeling of career failure with many years of bad managers and their unfulfilled promises and it is not hard to understand why many older employees feel an alienation from the institution to which they have dedicated much of their adult lives.

The Older, Cynical Employee

The negative attitude of older employees is humorously demonstrated in the comment of an older supervisor who attended one of my training programs. After I used an illustration in my program about the teamwork of Canadian geese by their use of a V-shaped flying formation and how this demonstrated teamwork and synergy, I saw him smile broadly in the back of the room. At the break, he came up to me, formed a V with his hands, and told me that his agency was like the geese. I knew from his mischievous expression that he had something other than teamwork in mind. I asked him in what way was working in his agency like the geese and their flying formation. Still making the V with his hands, he grinned and replied, "Because you spend most of your time looking at assholes."

Another issue that may contribute to this resentment and cynicism is that their older employees' personal lives are often in trouble. Years of shift work, working holidays, and other negative aspects of being in law enforcement have often wreaked havoc on family and social relationships. As Kevin Gilmartin describes in *Emotional Survival for Law Enforcement*, many of these relational failures were due to the person's overinvestment in the law enforcement career and emotional detachment from family and friends. Unfortunately, many employees blame these interpersonal failures on the agency.

> Leadership is practiced not so much in words as in attitude and in actions.
> —Harold S. Geneen

Whatever the causes, older employees may be a formidable impediment to a leader's attempts to implement change. These employees have heard the promises and programs of the past yet seen few, if any, positive changes. As they prepare to retire in the coming years, they will often emotionally give up on the agency, or their resentment may result in full-blown attacks against reforms and suggestions. As with the younger employees, they can be won over, but it will not be an easy task.

Diversity

When I first entered law enforcement in 1972, it was still staffed primarily by white males. Since that time, the profession has become much more diversified, with women and minorities now filling positions as police officers, managers, and executives. Though some police officers and managers still resist this diversity, these biased individuals are rare in my experience. If a white male manager or employee displays resentment toward others, he generally resents everyone and everything, not just women and minorities. Two issues, however, have raised the emotional stakes within the organizational culture—the *accusations of racial profiling* and the *impact of affirmative action*.

Racial profiling, the belief that law enforcement tends to target minorities for arrest and for traffic citations, has received national press and numerous comments by politicians and law enforcement executives. Though some individuals have certainly integrated their prejudices into their operational duties, the vast majority of law enforcement personnel resent accusations that they target certain categories of people for arrest. Given that most felony arrests are initiated by a citizen's or a victim's complaint, the race of the offender is decided before the police officer or deputy arrives on the scene. If an African American male committed an armed robbery, and his description is disseminated to responding officers, would it make good sense to stop and question Hispanic or Caucasian males? Crime data show that young minority males are often disproportionately arrested as violent offenders—because they disproportionately commit violent crimes (and are overwhelmingly the victims of violent crime).

This operational issue is important to law enforcement leaders because failing to address this issue *honestly* will affect their credibility with the rank and file. Law enforcement officers will readily support discipline when an individual misuses his or her authority against certain categories of people. The rank and file, however, are offended when managers imply to the public that this problem is widespread or when personnel are forced to go through meaningless new policies and procedures because a law enforcement executive wants to appease the media and local politicians. Political correctness without substantiation is not valued by the law enforcement organizational culture. Managers who easily succumb to this philosophy will likely not win the respect of the personnel within an agency, regardless of race or gender.

Affirmative action is another polarizing issue, one that is obviously more directly related to the internal culture of the agency. How leaders attempt to build a diverse workforce and management staff is another litmus test of how they are perceived by the rank and file. Though the goal of having a diverse workforce and management team is essential in today's society, how an agency responds to achieving this goal can be either unifying or destructive to the organizational culture.

> *Promoting individuals who are marginal employees or failing to confront problem employees simply because they are minority or female violates foundational leadership principles of fairness and accountability.*

Promoting individuals who are marginal employees or failing to confront problem employees simply because they are minority or female violates foundational leadership principles of fairness and accountability. These misguided approaches to handling diversity not only fail to demonstrate leadership, they will likely exacerbate racial and gender issues in the agency culture.

Though diversity is a complicated issue for American policing, law enforcement managers must analyze their thoughts on this potentially divisive topic and be able to articulate and defend their beliefs about the issue. When attempting to develop a rational and fair approach, leaders might look at an organizational culture that has handled the minority question in a rather exemplary manner—the American military. As an institution with likely the most diverse representation of American culture, it has approached this difficult issue through effective leadership, team building, and accountability—not special programs and dual standards. As a culture similar to that of the military, American policing should perhaps examine this successful approach to an emotionally charged issue.

Unions and Employee Groups

I have little work experience with police unions or employee bargaining groups. Most of my law enforcement experience has been in a state that did not permit collective bargaining for public employees, so I have little to offer in this area from personal experience. I have spent lots of time training and consulting in agencies with unions and employee groups, however, so I can reasonably suggest that these groups can have a strong impact on the internal organizational culture.

Poor leadership practices in American police history have often promoted the development of unions and collective bargaining, but what is the role of unions in the twenty-first century? I have seen these groups approach leadership in the police organization in one of two ways. In a positive model, more often seen in Canadian police agencies, unions work closely with organizational leadership on common goals, such as proper compensation, benefits, and disciplinary procedures. There also appears to be a consensus between the two groups about the necessity of dealing with destructive and unethical employees and with poor management practices.

> *Wars may be fought with weapons, but they are won by men. It is the spirit of the men who follow and of the man who leads that gains the victory.*
>
> —George S. Patton

Other unions appear to use the opposite approach, viewing their relationship with the agency hierarchy as purely adversarial. I have seen unions defend employees clearly unfit for duty and fight the organization's attempt to implement programs because managers have

diversity

unions and
employee groups

cynicism

occupational focus only
on bad behavior

clashing perspectives
between younger
and older employees

ineffective managers

bad managers

**Organizational
Culture**

proposed the changes and 5 percent of the officers don't want them. For managers in an agency with this clearly adversarial relationship between unions and management, this situation is a potential obstacle to implementing positive leadership strategies within the organizational culture. A friend of mine once remarked that some unions, because of this adversarial relationship, don't want good leadership in the agency. He felt that good leadership could reduce the influence and power of some unions, so they would likely criticize and resist even beneficial changes. As with the older employee, however, the only way leaders can win this battle with the unions is to prove by their ongoing actions and values that their leadership is not a gimmick.

The only way leaders can win this battle with the unions is to prove by their ongoing actions and values that their leadership is not a gimmick.

Bad and Ineffective Managers

Your biggest problem in attempting to implement the leadership strategies in this book will likely come from fellow managers and supervisors who have failed to demonstrate leadership. This stumbling block will arise in two ways. First, bad or ineffective managers will have created a substantiated cynicism toward leadership strategies in the culture. When I have asked law enforcement personnel what percentage of their past and current supervisors and managers have displayed true leadership behaviors, what do you think is their answer to this important question? 60 percent? 45 percent? 25 percent? Not even close. *Most respond 5–10 percent!* What this percentage means is that, actually or perceived, most managers are not good leaders, and their management failures have created a justifiable cynicism

> *Most managers are not good leaders, and their management failures have created a justifiable cynicism about anyone's attempt to practice good leadership.*

about anyone's attempt to practice good leadership. Conversely, and optimistically, leadership behaviors that are practiced daily will likely be noticed by personnel because the behaviors are so rare. An old biblical proverb states that to a starving man, anything tastes good. With these failures in the minds of employees, the shortcomings of your colleagues and predecessors will make principled leadership practices much more powerful in the organizational culture.

The other manner in which bad or ineffective managers might hamper good leadership strategies will come directly from the managers themselves. My experience and observations have been that someone who attempts to practice proactive leadership strategies makes bad or ineffective managers uncomfortable, if not downright hostile. Why? Because good leadership makes their lack of leadership skills much more apparent. Let me give you an example. Suppose you have decided to discipline a chronic problem employee, one who has been troublesome for every manager and supervisor in your agency. Supervisors and managers will affirm to you that this person has been a terrible problem. When you begin to build your case against the employee, however, what will you find in his or her personnel file? You will likely find not only that these same supervisors and managers failed to write up disciplinary reports or problems, but that they have given the employee good evaluations! These managers took the path of least resistance and failed to do what they knew they should do. Your attempts to realistically evaluate or correctively discipline employees will often bring attention (especially if there is some type of grievance hearing or process) to the previous supervisors' failures to handle the problem employee.

What Causes Stress in Law Enforcement?

I did a series of interviews in eight different agencies with personnel, both sworn and civilian. In more than one thousand interviews, I asked how long they had worked in the agency. Once I heard the answer, I asked if they had ever not wanted to come to work, if they ever wished they could quit. Over 90 percent replied "yes" to that question. When I asked why they had wanted to quit, an overwhelming number described a bad manager they were working for at the time. Very few listed operational danger, salary and benefits, or other issues that most police chiefs and sheriffs identify as the source of low morale or employee turnover.

But what makes a leader fail or succeed? Various behaviors, both positive and negative, are common among law enforcement managers around the country. The next chapter examines the typical destructive and neglectful actions that most law enforcement managers use in their daily contact with police officers, deputies, and civilian personnel. On a more positive note, however, the chapter also examines the behaviors of managers who have chosen the path of a leader.

The Seven Laws of Leadership

Law enforcement managers around the country handle their duties within the agency culture using many common methods. The concept of leadership must be understood in the context of what is actually happening in the daily lives of law enforcement managers and personnel, not what we wish were happening. What does leadership really look like in the law enforcement culture, and what does it look like when there is a failure to demonstrate it? As you read this chapter, look into your own past and compare your experiences to those of others.

Three Types of Managers

I often ask participants in management training programs to do a short written exercise, which you might find helpful to do as well. The exercise basically asks them to respond to two questions:

"Who is the best leader you have ever worked for? What characteristics or behaviors made you select this person as the best?"

"Who is the worst leader you have ever worked for? What characteristics or behaviors made you select this person as the worst?"

Over the years, thousands of supervisors and managers, representing federal, state, and local law enforcement agencies as well as police organizations from other countries, have responded to these two questions in remarkably similar ways. These similarities seem to fall naturally into categories that describe three types of managers—leaders, evil managers, and ineffective and unskilled managers. Further, from the respondents' descriptions of managers, seven "laws" of leadership have evolved. First, let's look at the three categories into which managers generally fall.

Leaders tend to generate commitment in most people they supervise. They lead by example, both professionally and personally. Though they fail on occasion, overall they consistently discipline themselves to demonstrate recognized leadership behaviors in their dealings with others. They are well known and respected among the rank and file in the agency, though they will often generate resentment or opposition among the organizational hierarchy. When I ask class attendees to estimate the percentage of law enforcement managers who are leaders, most indicate that *leaders make up 10 percent or less of managers within the law enforcement culture.*

Evil managers are the antithesis of their leader counterparts. They are consistently destructive to the organizational culture and to employees, and they are widely distrusted and despised throughout the agency. They are egotistical and self-centered, and they have a predatory perspective on others. They may have strong ethical and character problems and often engage in inappropriate behavior, such as sexual harassment, racism, and even corruption. When asked to estimate evil managers' presence among law enforcement managers, most respondents stated that *10 percent or less of managers are evil.*

The final group may be the most critical to examine more closely, since most of us likely fall into this category. *Ineffective managers* are individuals who are basically ethical and caring people like their leader counterparts; however, they do not consistently practice and demonstrate good leadership behavior with their subordinates. They are not disliked by the rank and file, but neither are they respected. They are perceived by most as wishy washy and inconsistent. Employees cannot trust them to stand behind them. This inconsistency is also seen in their fight-or-flight emotional makeup—they can be either very angry or upset at times or withdrawn emotionally or operationally from people and the law enforcement mission. By mathematical necessity, *close to 80 percent of law enforcement managers are viewed as unskilled or ineffective!*

The Seven Laws of Leadership

These categories of managers (and the leadership strategies detailed in later chapters) are best understood by examining how the behaviors and characteristics of each type of manager differ in light of the seven laws of leadership.

> *You learn far more from negative leadership than from positive leadership. Because you learn how not to do it. And, therefore, you learn how to do it.*
> —**Norman Schwarzkopf**

These seven laws represent categories of issues and manager characteristics identified most frequently by the law enforcement managers I have surveyed.

The Seven Laws of Leadership

> **Law 1** > *Integrity and honor*

Given that American policing is tasked with enforcing the laws of the United States, it is not surprising that personnel within the culture place a high premium on *integrity*. **Leaders**, those admired by the respondents, are seen as possessing moral authority; they are ethical, and their lives model integrity. Though much of the debate about ethics often involves legal integrity (not committing crimes or corruption), most respondents focused on *interpersonal* integrity, such as being honest in one's dealings with others. The leader is perceived as leading by example and consistently telling the truth. Employees always know where they stand with this individual—in positive and in negative feedback situations. One of the key elements of integrity and honor that was often listed was standing up for employees, even if politically or organizationally it was a dangerous thing for the leader to do. Integrity demonstrated by backing up employ-

> *Integrity demonstrated by backing up employees is highly valued because it is probably viewed as courage, a critical value within a warrior-class culture like law enforcement.*

ees is highly valued because it is probably viewed as courage, a critical value within a warrior-class culture like law enforcement. The bottom line is that personnel always perceive a leader as being someone trustworthy—both ethically and interpersonally.

The integrity of **evil managers** is obviously diametrically different from that of their leader counterparts. Evil managers are perceived as unethical and as regularly circumventing rules (and the law) to suit their personal agenda. The most common remark made in this category concerned lying: you cannot trust this person to tell the truth to you, the courts, or the law enforcement organization. This person is also seen as a back stabber and as one who will punish you for doing something he or she regularly does. In other words, the evil manager models "do as I say, not as I do."

Ineffective managers' integrity is seen as in between the

integrity of leaders and evil managers. Though most managers are
seen as generally ethical in a legal
sense, many are often seen as com-
promising interpersonally in their
dealings with employees. They are
perceived as unreliable in their
defense of employees, tending to
make decisions that are politically
expedient. They cannot be trusted to
stand behind employees if things get rocky.
They are also perceived as telling people what
they want to hear and not letting employees
know where they stand.

> *The glue that holds all relationships together—including the relationship between the leader and the led—is trust, and trust is based on integrity.*
>
> **—Brian Tracy**

Law 2 > *Servanthood*

The next category of behaviors and traits has to
do with how managers seem to perceive *their* role
with others and within the organization. **Leaders** are
described as servants to others, to the
organization, and to the law enforcement
profession and mission. They are perceived
as being unselfish and not taking themselves or their rank
or position too seriously. They work as team members—*with*
people rather than over them. One of the most common
statements describing this servant perspective is "they would
never ask me to do anything they would not do themselves."
They are also described as never taking credit for others'
accomplishments but always taking responsibility when
things go wrong. Basically, the leader is seen as an individual who consistently places others and the mission ahead of
his or her own personal needs.

Evil managers, conversely, are described as egotistical,
self-centered, and prideful, taking themselves and their position or rank very seriously. They are seen as talking down to
subordinates, willing to help others only if it serves their
own agenda, and often manipulative of people and events
for their benefit. They seem always to be seeking more power

and recognition, taking credit for others' accomplishments but never the blame for what they do wrong. They are perceived as sacrificing the agency and the law enforcement mission for their own interests.

Ineffective managers are perceived as unselfish to some degree but always looking out for their own interests in conflicts between their careers and reputations and those of employees. They are generally seen as helpful and supportive of employees—but only if it does not get them into trouble with upper management. They are often described as being unable to make decisions because of their fear of getting in trouble. This fear of making a decision seems to prevent them from being proactive operationally or standing behind staff when something goes wrong. They are also described as micromanagers of unimportant matters yet withdrawn from employees, both operationally and interpersonally.

Law 3　　Mentorship

The next category of responses concerns how managers regard their roles as *developers and teachers* of others—how they view the mistakes and the successes of their subordinates. **Leaders** are perceived as caring for and believing in their personnel, and wanting them to improve. They are regarded as mentors who view mistakes as part of the learning process yet also encourage exemplary work. They pay attention to each employee's performance and career in the agency. They make employees feel important and valued, and they treat every person fairly. They care for the well-being of employees, both professionally and personally. Many respondents comment that leaders care not only for the employee but also for the employee's family and off-duty achievements and tragedies.

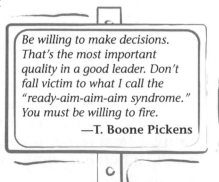

> Be willing to make decisions. That's the most important quality in a good leader. Don't fall victim to what I call the "ready-aim-aim-aim syndrome." You must be willing to fire.
>
> —**T. Boone Pickens**

> An empowered organization is one in which individuals have the knowledge, skill, desire, and opportunity to personally succeed in a way that leads to collective organizational success.
>
> —Stephen R. Covey

Evil managers are seen as caring only for themselves and as viewing everyone as a problem, a potential threat, or a tool to further their careers. They are categorized as constantly searching for weaknesses and mistakes in others that they can exploit for their own benefit. Evil managers are viewed as enforcers—only interacting to punish employees for mistakes. They are also seen as vindictive in their dealings with others.

Ineffective managers generally seem to view employees as potential sources of getting them in trouble. These managers give the impression that they are more concerned about employees making mistakes than about them being operationally proactive or proficient. They are seen as aloof, taking little if any interest in their staffs' careers and professional development, except those employees who are favorites—either their friends or those who stroked their egos. To these individuals, ineffective managers demonstrate blatant (at least in everyone else's view) favoritism when awarding perks and making disciplinary decisions.

Law 4 ▷ *Professionalism*

While Law 3 pertains to how managers view the careers of others, Law 4 pertains to the *professional expertise and skills (or lack thereof) of managers*. **Leaders** are seen as skilled professionals who consistently learn new skills necessary for the job and for their roles as leaders. They are perceived as having a high regard for training and are described as lifelong learners—always up-to-date on their knowledge and skills. They also demonstrate this interest in learning by always being willing to listen to others' opinions and input and to implement new ideas. Finally, they are described as never managing from behind a desk. As a result, they are seen as operationally involved and leading from out front—they are still cops, not forgetting or forsaking their law enforcement roots.

> *Management is efficiency in climbing the ladder of success; leadership determines whether the ladder is leaning against the right wall.*
>
> —**Stephen R. Covey**

Evil managers seem to believe that training and education are useless. They give the impression that they know all the skills based on common sense and generally prefer the old way of doing things. Evil managers are described as dinosaurs (one cop told me he felt he worked at Jurassic Park) who are threatened by individuals who have education or professional expertise. Evil managers give the impression that they are never wrong, yet employees describe them as lazy and uninvolved. If these managers are seen operationally, they are usually trying to catch employees doing something wrong or are using their operational duties to get free perks (such as coffee and meals) or for more serious graft and corruption.

Ineffective managers are usually interested in training programs but are seen to focus on administrative and specialized training that will help them move up the organizational ladder. Because they do not mingle with the staff, they are not popular with the rank and file. They tend to concentrate on their technical, administrative, or political skills (brown nosing) and rarely become involved in operational duties. They are perceived as having lost their cop perspective and are often described as desk jockeys. Many respondents believe that ineffective managers get promoted, such as to police chief, more often than leaders in the agency.

Law 5 > **Positive attitude, emotions, and temperament**

This category of management survey responses focuses on the *emotional and mental attitude* that individuals display when carrying out their management and operational duties. **Leaders** are perceived as generally positive about the organizational mission and about employees in general. They still have senses of humor and do not take themselves or the daily crises too seriously. They are described as emotionally stable—always calm and predictable in their ability to handle issues. If they have a bad day or are confronted by their superiors, the rank and file do not pay the consequences. They are seen as thermostats, individuals who set the emotional temperature of the environment when things become stressful. Most respondents attribute this emotional stability to leaders' skills in dealing with others and to their operational expertise. This combination of skill and experience reduces their tendency to get upset when things go wrong.

> Leaders are seen as thermostats, individuals who set the emotional temperature of the environment when things become stressful.

> Leadership is a matter of having people look at you and gain confidence, seeing how you react. If you're in control, they're in control.
> —Tom Landry

Evil managers, interestingly enough, are also described as not being very emotional. This lack of emotion, however, is attributed to their tendency to be consistently negative about the agency, the mission, and people in general so that they are not surprised when things go wrong. They find fault with everything and everyone, and they will always find something to criticize about an act of heroism or successful investigation or arrest. Their anger is calculated, not emotional. They do not get mad, they get even. They are known to use gossip and rumors to stir things up and actually seem to enjoy a crisis, problem, or controversy.

Ineffective managers are the most emotional and inconsistent. Because of their personal agenda and lack of rapport with the rank and file, they respond emotionally when things go wrong—often with angry outbursts. They are often described as changing from day to day, which makes them hard to trust to do the right thing.

Emotional Responses of the Ineffective Manager

When I am explaining emotional fight-or-flight examples of ineffective managers and their inability to demonstrate leadership, two illustrations always come to mind. One sergeant told me that his supervisor (a lieutenant) always got angry when something went wrong or when anyone simply asked a question. The supervisor's tendency to blow up earned him the nickname C4. Another supervisor attending training stated that his supervisor changed his mind and his approach to leadership daily. This supervisor earned the nickname Sybil (from a book about a woman with multiple personalities). Employees' first task every morning at work was to figure out which version of the supervisor had shown up that day.

Law 6   *Reinforcement and accountability*

This next law, or principle, stems from how managers view the role of *rewards and discipline* in the organizational culture. **Leaders** are seen as balancing encouragement and accountability. They consistently recognize exemplary behavior but also respond to marginal and unwanted behavior. They reward good employees verbally (in speech or in writing) or with an award or other tangible display of achievement, and they confront and document the behaviors of problem and marginal employees. They are seen as clear in their expectations of others and of the work product and are viewed as fair and consistent in reinforcing these expectations with both rewards and discipline.

Evil managers are described as seeing their role solely as enforcers—to punish and catch staff doing something wrong. They seem pleased when they can discipline someone and enjoy punishing employees. They do not believe in rewards and encouragement—employees are just doing what they are paid to do. As previously mentioned, they are also seen as going out of their way to find fault with commendable behavior.

> *The art of leading, in operations large or small, is the art of dealing with humanity, of working diligently on behalf of men, of being sympathetic with them, but equally, of insisting that they make a square facing toward their own problems.*
>
> —S. L. A. Marshall

Ineffective managers are inconsistent in terms of accountability. They are either unskilled or unsure about how to deal with problem employees, so they don't have the courage or skill to confront them and do not do so. If they do respond to a problem, they generally do it through a vague letter or a policy that punishes everyone for the behavior of an individual. Since they don't spend time with many employees, their reward systems are usually confined to their favorites; they often don't even know about the exemplary behavior of most employees.

Law 7   *Proactive communication*

The role of *interpersonal skills* is the subject of this final law—how managers use (or fail to use) the power of communication. **Leaders** are seen as masters of communication—verbal and nonverbal, and in their ability and willingness to listen. They are described as consistently in touch with staff and always approachable. They are also seen as skilled in their ability to observe and interpret verbal and nonverbal behaviors in others. This emotional and social intelligence gives them the ability to interact, resolve problems, and encourage and mentor others. They use communication and listening skills to interact consistently with those around them—both with staff and with the public.

Evil managers are seen as communicating only to manipulate or destroy others. They are perceived as a type of social terrorist, a person who abuses others in person or behind their backs. They do not listen to others, but employees are usually afraid to talk to them anyway. They never solicit feedback—it is always one-way communication that seems to indicate "my way or no way." They generally use communication only as a weapon and are often engaged in spreading rumors and gossip to damage others.

> *All of life is a risk; in fact we're not going to get out alive. Casualness leads to casualties. Communication is the ability to affect other people with words.*
>
> —**Jim Rohn**

Though not as malevolent as their evil colleagues, **ineffective managers** are also poor communicators and listeners with most staff. Their absence from operational duties and their emotional inconsistency give them little rapport or trust with the rank and file. Sensing this alienation, ineffective managers often retreat further into their offices or into organizational politics, where they feel comfortable. Any communication with staff is usually confined to the few who are perceived as their favorites.

What is striking about the descriptions of managers in our agencies and the laws of leadership that emerge from these descriptions is that nothing remarkable or new is revealed. All of us can identify names with the three types of managers and can cite personal examples of poor communicators and good communicators. There is more to this discussion, however, than rehashing war stories of good leaders and bad managers. Consider an important question: If I asked the absolute worst manager you ever worked for to describe his or her best leader and worst manager, would the answers and descriptions be different? No, the manager would list the same characteristics of leadership and poor management that you and others did. So a more important question might be, if everyone knows what leadership is like and what behaviors are always a sign of *not* being a leader, why are most managers failing?

Self-Awareness

Early in my training career, I walked into a classroom and was greeted by a sight I will never forget. Sitting in the classroom were the three worst law enforcement managers I had ever worked for. These men were legends in my former police department. They were incompetent; they ridiculed officers in front of other personnel; and they never confronted marginal behavior or affirmed positive behavior. I was shocked to the point that I walked back out of the classroom, where the course coordinator noticed my perplexed expression and asked me what was the matter. When I told him, he simply responded, "So what?" I jokingly told him that half my illustrations of bad managers were sitting in the classroom, so this was destined to be a brief lecture.

The real reason I was worried, however, was twofold. First, I thought that when I used illustrations in my program that included experiences I'd had with them, they would recognize themselves in these scenarios and be offended. Second, since their management styles at my former agency violated most of the leadership principles we would discuss that day, I assumed they would naturally argue with me in class about the validity of these principles in a law enforcement agency. After all, anyone who had worked for these individuals would believe that these three men disagreed with recognized and established methods of leading others.

During the next eight hours, I was to get an education in human behavior. They loved the course! They came up to me at the end of the day and told me how much they had enjoyed the lecture. Then, grinning, they told me that when I had talked about bad managers, they knew I was talking about two men in their department who were not in class that day. They ended with this statement: "It is too bad those guys couldn't have been in class to hear this—they sure need to." I was stunned. They had not seen themselves in any of the scenarios I had used. They had also failed to see their own lives as violating any of the principles of leadership and had instead projected failure to other supervisors. They had also communicated that they believed in the leadership principles the course espoused. At the time, I did not understand what was happening. Later, after many more training programs and tenure in a leadership position in another law enforcement agency, I saw that this lack of self-awareness in managers was very common, if not universal.

Why do bright, often educated managers fail to follow principles they believe in and can articulate? With 90 percent of managers failing, the next chapter may be the most important one in this book. It may also be the most difficult for any of us to accept.

Why Most Managers Are Ineffective

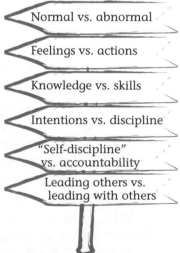

Of the three types of managers law enforcement personnel identify in their agencies (leaders, evil managers, and ineffective managers), ineffective managers are the most common (perceived as 80 percent of all managers). These managers seem to care for the agency and their employees but don't seem to carry out these good intentions through actions that build commitment in the agency. Given that these 80 percent are not usually bad, uneducated, or untrained individuals, maybe the answer to why they are ineffective lies with their misconceptions about themselves, others, or the concept of leadership in general.

Leadership Paradigms

Examining common paradigms, or belief systems, about leadership and about human nature might help reveal these misconceptions so that we can determine if these belief systems are really grounded in reality. These perspectives will enable us to examine why many of us are not effective as leaders and will also be the foundation of many of the solutions and proactive strategies discussed in the next chapters of

Normal vs. abnormal

Feelings vs. actions

Knowledge vs. skills

Intentions vs. discipline

"Self-discipline" vs. accountability

Leading others vs. leading with others

this book. Six paradigms in particular may help us discover why we are often ineffective as leaders.

Paradigm 1   *Normal versus abnormal behavior*

This first paradigm may be the most important and is based on our beliefs about human nature in general. Are we naturally prone to leadership? Is it normal, or naturally within most human beings, to look out for the welfare of others, deal with difficult issues, and practice the behaviors exhibited by effective leaders that were listed in the previous chapter? Conversely, is it abnormal, or unnatural, for individuals to demonstrate the behaviors of the ineffective or evil managers when they are selfish, self-centered, and hesitant to confront problem employees? Basically, what I am asking you to consider is whether human behavior is naturally good or bad.

Maybe we should let our children help us answer this question. If you have raised children, you have likely had to confront them or discipline them when they were very young. Why? Were they being too nice to their siblings, too respectful to you or your spouse, or too prone to clean up their toys when asked? Not if your kids were like mine. At a very young age, they displayed self-centeredness, stubbornness, and even a tendency to assault others when angry—behaviors that were generally not demonstrated by their parents. Two-year-olds, for example, are a high-maintenance group—you have to watch them constantly and monitor their behavior. If you were a remotely decent parent, you had to discipline and train your children to share, not to hit others, and to control their behaviors.

It should be obvious from my previous comments that I believe we are naturally selfish and self-centered. It is our nature to look to our own needs first. If you have been in the law enforcement profession, I do not have to evangelize to you about human nature; you have seen it in its purest and most negative forms. Understanding that we do not naturally want to do the right thing is critical to our understanding of ourselves and to the concept of leadership in general. I propose that leaders are abnormal. They act contrary to their own human nature. If that is not true, then why are only 10 percent of us perceived as effective leaders and the rest of us either ineffective or evil? If leadership is normal human nature, then why aren't most of us doing it correctly and consistently?

> *Many people equate good management with perfection. This is a fallacy. If perfection could be achieved, there would be no need for management.*
>
> —James L. Hayes

Further evidence that leadership is not normal behavior is that law enforcement agencies generally do not react against poor management. Let's be honest. If someone is a terrible manager (and nearly everyone in the organization agrees with this assessment), the average law enforcement agency does not seem motivated to confront this person. Managers and executives respond by saying, "That's just the way Larry is," and ignore his ineffectiveness, even if he is having a negative impact on the organization. Conversely, if a manager is popular with the rank and file, the normal organizational response to this positive sign of leadership is not affirmation. Many agency managers and executives are threatened by anyone's reputation as a leader and often respond negatively. An individual who practices the positive attributes of leadership described in the seven laws of leadership (see page 29) will generally be unsupported, if not outright opposed. I believe this typical agency response to ineffective managers and to leaders demonstrates that leadership is abnormal behavior.

Paradigm 2 ▷ **Feelings and emotions versus skills and actions**

This important paradigm may help explain why most managers who are ineffective do not realize that they are failing. It may also clarify why when managers who hear my lectures invite me to train supervisors at their agencies, their subordinates routinely tell me that the managers do not demonstrate most of the principles discussed in these programs. Why would managers invite me to lecture others about concepts they don't practice? *Because they think and believe they do—even if they don't.* I am convinced that most of us fall into this trap because we confuse *beliefs and feelings with skills and actions.*

> *Why would managers invite me to lecture others about concepts they don't practice? Because they think and believe they do—even if they don't.*

I think that most of us are unaware of our shortcomings—we do not see ourselves as we really are. What helps us tolerate this lack of congruence between who we think we are and how we actually behave is likely our natural tendency to rationalize our behavior by assuming that agreeing with good leadership principles is the same as doing them. I heard a great quotation from an instructor (a saying of uncertain origin and many variations) that summarizes this tendency toward self-deception:

> *"We judge ourselves by our motives but others by their actions."*

If we are honest with ourselves, we know this is true. We tend to be aware of others' mistakes but naturally fail to see our own faults. We *must* understand that we cannot trust our own perception of how we are doing as a leader, parent, or spouse.

Those managers who ask me to train their agency supervisors in strategies they do not practice themselves genuinely like and agree with the principles of the training program, which they *assume* they are doing. This self-deception occurs in areas other than leadership. I have met many spouses and parents who are devastated when their mate or children express criticism or beliefs that they are not being effective. These spouses and parents will generally say in their defense that they love their spouse and their children and cannot understand why their loved ones think that way. Now, if you ask them whether they routinely spend time with their spouse or children and whether they communicate effectively, they will begin to get flustered and say, "But I have a very demanding job" or "I am very tired when I get home." They do not instinctively understand that feelings and emotions are not the same as skills and actions.

Paradigm 3 > *Knowledge versus skills*

Our effectiveness as leaders is influenced not only by our understanding of the role of self-deception, but also by our *skill levels* and *prior learning*. Let me explain. Suppose I want to be a more effective leader by strengthening my interpersonal skills—I want to be a better listener and communicator. Now, suppose also that I have not had effective role models for these skills in either my family or work environment, nor have I been effectively trained in these skills. If an employee comes into my office to ask me a question, or if I must reprimand employees for their marginal performance, can I do it? If I sit behind my desk, cross my arms, and glance at my watch while the employee is talking with me, am I being effective? Our ability to practice and master appropriate leadership skills is based on our past development of skills. I am convinced that since most of us have not had a significant number of good role models in our personal and professional careers, we don't know what being effective *looks like.*

Compounding this role model problem is that we have received very little training in the emotional dimensions of dealing with others. As a result, we are unsure what to do in a given situation and will either not perform the task effectively or ignore doing what we need to do because we are so uncomfortable or unskilled in critical interpersonal behaviors.

A friend of mine who is an effective counselor and therapist tells me that most marriages are in trouble because the couple assumes that marriage is based on love, an emotion, that the marriage will be successful because they love their spouse or potential spouse. He adds that they don't understand that marriage is a skill, and that most of us come into a relationship without the prerequisite modeling, training, or skills to be effective. A quote he gave me illustrates this relationship between emotion and skill:

> *"We live as fully as we love and have the skills
> to do so."*

Given the current divorce rate and numbers of bad marriages, this statement may have a lot of truth to it.

In the same way, leadership requires managing our time, dealing with angry employees, and using a multitude of skills that many of us have never been trained to do nor seen modeled correctly by our own supervisors and managers. If we do not know how to do these important tasks, we are likely to fail. This problem is why effective training (especially in the people skills) is important for those who will be effective as leaders.

Paradigm 4 ▷ Normal intentions versus abnormal discipline

If you have followed my logic thus far, and you agree that leadership is abnormal behavior that is not based solely on emotions and feelings, and that you must have the necessary skills to pull it off, what else would you guess is necessary to becoming an effective leader? I am convinced it is the intrapersonal skill of *discipline*. Because leadership is abnormal behavior, we have to force ourselves to be leaders by making ourselves do the right thing even when we don't feel like it. I think the number one difference between the leader and the ineffective manager is that leaders consistently do not allow themselves to act normally in situations when their basic human nature is to get angry, impatient, or take the path of least resistance. They have these normal emotions, but they resist and master them and do what they know they need to do even when they don't feel like it. Abraham Lincoln once commented on this role of discipline as it relates to our natural tendency to be lazy and self-centered:

> *"You cannot change human nature, but you can change
> human action."*

If I understand him correctly, he believed that leaders are not unselfish people but are selfish human beings who force themselves to do unselfish things. Ineffective managers, conversely, tend to give in to their natural tendencies and fail to demonstrate leadership consistently. They never, or rarely, put their good thoughts into action.

Let me give you an example. I believe that one of the more important and effective leadership practices is routinely spending time with each one of your employees, often in their operational duties. This concept of "management by walking around" (MBWA) has been repeatedly stressed in the leadership literature. What is interesting is that everyone agrees aloud (or by nodding) with this suggestion during training, but if you ask them individually if they regularly practice MBWA, they will admit that they rarely do it. This failure of managers to perform a widely recognized management strategy is confirmed by the rank and file, who comment that they generally never see managers or executives in their agencies during normal day-to-day duties.

> *Management is doing things right; leadership is doing the right things.*
> —**Peter Drucker**

Why do most of us fail to follow through on what we know are the right things to do? Because we do not discipline ourselves to do them when we are tired or unsure of how they will be perceived. If you ask managers why they don't practice MBWA, they will generally blame a busy work schedule or concerns that employees will think they are spying on them. When I propose that they might not be so busy if they were more in touch with their employees, or that employees' suspicions would diminish if the managers kept showing up, they agree. When I follow up with these managers later, however, they admit that they still do not spend time with employees. I think they are waiting to feel like it or for it to be convenient, which will likely be rarely, if at all. Leaders discipline themselves to show up even when they don't want to and dramatically affect their organizational culture as a result.

Paradigm 5 > **"Self-discipline" versus accountability**

If we are honest, most of us have to admit that we are not very disciplined. New Year's resolutions are generally not realized—most of us continue to be overweight and not exercise, and we don't develop the skills or habits we know are beneficial for us. With that in mind, how do we become disciplined to become abnormal? I am convinced that discipline is much more likely to become a reality if we have others or a system hold us accountable. When we know that we will pay consequences if we don't perform a task, we are much more likely to follow through and do it. If we have to pay consequences for not doing the right thing, we will generally force ourselves to be more conscientious and go against our basic lazy and self-indulgent nature.

> *I am convinced that discipline is much more likely to become a reality if we have others or a system hold us accountable.*

Accountability

As a professor in the university system and as an instructor in the law enforcement academy, I have taught many classes to students in academic and training environments. Now, predict the reaction of most students if I told them at the beginning of class that there would be no tests or examinations of any type and that everyone would receive a passing grade regardless of effort. Would they read the materials, attend class, listen in class, and take notes? Some of them would (likely about 10 percent) but what would the remaining 90 percent do? They would give in to their natural tendencies not to take the class seriously and not do the assigned readings or attend class. It is critical to note that these are not bad individuals. They are just going to do what comes naturally and take the path of least resistance. If, however, they have a

> test on the materials and lectures every week, most of these same individuals will attend and be attentive in class. What is the key difference in the performance of the same students in these two different scenarios? *The difference is accountability.*

As an example of this concept and its application to law enforcement leadership, let's suppose we are evaluated monthly by employees on whether we routinely practice MBWA in operational duties, and this evaluation is used by our superiors to determine merit raises and promotional opportunities. Would we be more likely to practice management by walking around? Absolutely! Accountability makes us more likely to do the right thing; it makes us discipline ourselves to go against our natural tendencies to be lazy and distracted. If you want to be "abnormal" and an effective leader, you cannot generally do it without others holding you accountable. If you really think about it, for most of us, the concept of self-discipline is probably not a reality.

Paradigm 6 — *Leading others versus leading with others*

This paradigm relates to the power of peer support. Just as we are more disciplined when we are held accountable, I believe that we also tend to show discipline consistently when we tackle problems and tasks with others. When we are asked to do a task alone, especially one that is difficult, we easily become apprehensive and perform it incorrectly or not at all. If we have to counsel an aggressive employee who will likely file a grievance, we will naturally feel

> *Just as we are more disciplined when we are held accountable, I believe that we also tend to show discipline consistently when we tackle problems and tasks with others.*

nervous or threatened by the meeting even if we have been trained in the legal and policy requirements of employee discipline. This uncertainty may provoke fight-or-flight behavior so that we either overstate or understate the issue in the meeting or opt not to have the meeting at all. If, however, we include another supervisor (especially one who is skilled in this area), we will more likely have the meeting and feel more comfortable and skilled in our counseling session. Why? Because we tend to be more positively influenced and courageous (a critical leadership skill) when we know we are not alone and when we are being observed by someone we respect.

How many times have you faced a difficult task, like the employee-counseling scenario, with reservations about having to do it? Next time you feel this apprehension, approach another supervisor whom you respect, outline your intentions and strategy, and ask, "Do you think this is a good idea?" When this person agrees with you (not giving you information, just affirmation), you are much more likely to perform the task. Why? Because the supervisor will have given you emotional support, and if you do not have the counseling session, he or she may ask you about it later, and you will be embarrassed that you did not follow through (going back to the issue of accountability in Paradigm 5). We often regard peer pressure as being negative, but it can have a strong positive influence on human behavior as well.

Where Do We Go from Here?

Many paradigms and principles help explain why most of us are not effective as leaders. Leadership is an abnormal behavior that requires skills and discipline, which are usually the result of accountability and the assistance of others. Understanding and even fully accepting why we are ineffective, however, does not necessarily translate into changed behavior. Fortunately, there are many practical ways to operationalize these dimensions in our daily management duties. Though the task of becoming abnormal may seem overwhelming, remember that even if you make only small positive changes in your leadership skills, these changes will likely have a strong influence on those around you. After all, you have very little competition—only 10 percent of your peers are successful leaders!

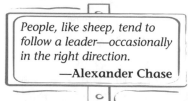

People, like sheep, tend to follow a leader—occasionally in the right direction.

—Alexander Chase

Developing Intrapersonal Skills

Managing yourself is the foundation for becoming an effective leader in the law enforcement culture. If you cannot master yourself, you cannot lead others. Few would deny that the most effective leaders in our lives led by example; their lives and actions spoke louder than their words.

Warnings for the Would-Be Leader

Anyone reading the above sentences will find themselves affirming that principle, but I must warn you that ineffec-

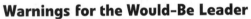

tive managers around us agree with this principle as well. Therefore, heed the following warnings or you risk intellectually agreeing with the leadership principles yet not demonstrating these principles to others in your everyday life.

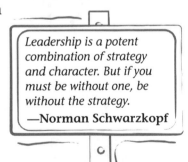

Leadership is a potent combination of strategy and character. But if you must be without one, be without the strategy.

—Norman Schwarzkopf

Five Warnings

Warning 1 > **Don't trust yourself.**

Self-deception has such a strong pull on all of our lives that we cannot rely on our own opinions of how we are doing. To demonstrate this, I assure you that you did something that we all do when discussing ineffective managers. When I teach classes, I always ask people sitting in the audience to tell me why they believe most managers are ineffective and fail to be leaders. Without fail, everyone uses the pronoun "they" when responding to the question. They state things like, "They don't communicate," or, "They don't have enough courage." These same people had just agreed that 90 percent of managers are failing, yet they instinctively do not put themselves in the category of being ineffective. I am confident that you did the same when reading about ineffective managers. I do it, too.

A fellow trainer once told me that there is always a way for instructors to tell if they have reached and affected people in training classes on leadership. He said that if a participant comes up to you at a break or at the end of class and remarks on enjoying the program but adds that he or she wishes other supervisors or managers could have attended the training, then you have failed to teach that person effectively. As long as people project the need for leadership skills onto other people, they are incapable of learning to lead. This scenario is by far the most common reaction to training programs that I have conducted.

As long as people project the need for leadership skills onto other people, they are incapable of learning to lead.

My colleague added, however, that if a participant says the class was a reminder of how much he or she has fallen short of being a leader, then you have positively affected the person. This latter type of comment has been very rare in my training experience. The bottom line: your lack of self-awareness and an unrealistic view of your performance will always plague your ability to be a leader.

> **Warning 2** ⟩ ***The road to hell is paved with good intentions.***

One of the most remarkable things I have discovered in the last several years is that most managers have positive thoughts about and intentions toward their subordinates, but few of these managers follow through by putting these thoughts into actual comments or actions toward employees. Why? Because we get so busy in daily activities that we get distracted and forget to act on effective leadership principles that we *intend* to do. Let me give you a scenario that is likely acted out hundreds of times per day in every law enforcement agency in the United States.

Suppose one of your subordinates is injured in the line of duty or loses a family member to cancer. Most of us will instinctively think about calling to check on the employee or sending a note. What normally happens though? We get busy or distracted and forget about this potentially powerful act of leadership. The next thing we know, the employee is back at work and we never acted on our good thoughts. Not only did we fail to demonstrate leadership, the employee likely interpreted our lack of

> *Long is the way/ and hard, that out of hell leads up to light.*
>
> **—John Milton**

attention as a lack of care or concern for him or her individually. This interpretation is not really accurate, but the employee will believe it nonetheless. I believe that because of this lack of follow through, many managers are incorrectly labeled as not caring. Our failure to discipline ourselves to act on our good thoughts is one of the most serious problems that we must safeguard ourselves against. I think this failure is also behind much of our lack of self-awareness of how ineffective we are. After all, we *intended* to do the right thing!

> **Warning 3** ⟩ ***Good feelings usually come after, not before, obedience.***

We all put too much emphasis on *feeling* like doing what we know we should do. We know we should write up a problem employee, but we are tired and want to go home. We know we should spend time with our spouse and children when we get home, but we are tired of talking all day or dealing with issues, so we watch television instead. We all take the easy road, especially when we are tired. As a result, most of us are generally ineffective at work and at home. One of the ways to minimize this common mistake we all make is to understand that feelings generally come *after*, not before, obedience. Let's explore this important principle.

Many, if not most, Americans are overweight and out of shape. We don't feel like going on a diet or exercising. Several years ago, I (briefly) got into the best shape of my life and learned the valuable principle of delayed gratification. As I prepared to exercise, especially in the beginning, I dreaded it—it was not what I wanted to do. This feeling did not go away during exercise; I still didn't enjoy it. I noticed, however, that after I was through, I had a very satisfying feeling of accomplishment—I had conquered myself and done something that I had not wanted to do. Many of you have experienced that post-obedience satisfaction of exercise or dieting. Does this apply to management and family? Absolutely.

Gilmartin gives a great example of this principle in *Emotional Survival for Law Enforcement*. All of us love our children and agree that we should spend more time with them, but we generally don't follow through. Gilmartin believes that much of this failure is due to our emotional fatigue after getting off work—we don't feel like doing what we know we should do. He recommends that during your days off (when you are not emotionally tired), you sit down with a sheet of paper and schedule specific times during the week to spend time with your children. After scheduling these commitments, immediately go tell your family of your intentions (so you won't be able to back out). He promises that if you schedule to take your two kids to a movie on Tuesday evening, you won't feel like doing it on the way home from work Tuesday—you will be tired as you always are. You will have to go, however, because you told them beforehand, so you will regretfully take them to the movie. Though initially your attitude will not be positive, sometime during the movie, you will find that you actually enjoy being there with your kids—and they will appreciate your time with them. By the time you go home, you will be glad you did what you intended to do, even though you originally didn't feel like following through earlier that day.

The same principle applies at work. All of us agree we should spend time with subordinates when there is not a problem, yet few of us do it. Why? Because we wait to feel like it—which, given our busy schedules, will likely be never. So to overcome this, we should specifically schedule time with employees, tell them about it, and then show up *even if we cannot afford the time or are tired*. Even if employees don't immediately respond to these encounters (and they won't), we will know we have done the right thing. I think most of us put far too much emphasis on external rewards, thinking we need recognition and rewards from others. The greatest reward (and motivation), however, often comes from the *internal* satisfaction of knowing you have done the right thing—even when no one else recognizes or rewards it. I think all great athletes, and all great leaders, understand this principle of not letting our selfish desires get in the way of becoming what we can be.

> *We should specifically schedule time with employees, tell them about it, and then show up even if we cannot afford the time or are tired.*

Warning 4   **Don't expect affirmation from the agency or others for doing the right thing.**

One of the reasons Warning 3 is so important is that we will generally not be affirmed if we regularly practice leadership skills. You cannot depend on others in the organizational hierarchy to reinforce or reward your attempts at leadership. Why? As mentioned in chapter 4, the agency hierarchy will be suspicious of leadership because it exposes the actions of most managers as being wrong. If you consistently discipline problem employees, past managers who did not discipline these individuals will not be appreciative. You will be labeled as stirring up trouble and rocking the boat. You will also create work for upper management, who will have to deal with administrative work (such as grievances) when you hold employees accountable. Basically, leadership makes ineffective managers look bad, and your efforts will not be applauded by ineffective or evil managers (don't forget—they are 90 percent of the agency hierarchy). Line staff, with their jaded viewpoints and cynicism, will take potshots at your attempts to do the right thing, even if they agree with what you are doing.

> *Wise people, even though all laws were abolished, would still lead the same life.*
>
> —**Aristophanes**

Warning 5 ▷ *Don't try to do this alone.*
Though seemingly contradictory to Warnings 3 and 4, this warning is essential because of two sources of resistance—from yourself and from others. Because of our tendency toward self-deception, we need to ask others to hold us accountable and expose inconsistencies in our lives. If you ask your friends to give you feedback and confront you when you fail to demonstrate leadership, you will be more disciplined to be obedient. With personnel in the agency second-guessing and criticizing your attempts at leadership, seeking a few individuals to help keep you on track and provide *solicited* feedback—which always tends to be more genuine and unbiased than unasked-for opinions—is critical. We are social creatures, and the discipline of being leaders is greatly enhanced when we have others help us.

You may think that five warnings is overkill or a negative way to begin these chapters on leadership principles. Considering, however, that most managers are failing to lead within their organizational cultures, I cannot overemphasize that traditional leadership strategies alone do not seem to be working, even when the underlying principles are sound. Given that ineffective managers are often well-meaning and highly trained individuals, intellectually understanding leadership principles is obviously not the key to being effective. Besides, many of the suggestions in this book are common sense and in most management literature. The warnings are therefore meant to forge a mind-set of recognizing the extreme difficulty of applying the principles in work and home environments so that you are more likely to make a deliberate effort to act on what you learn.

Self-Management Principles

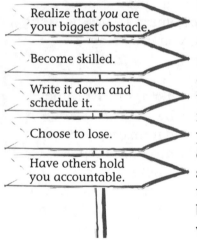

Realize that *you* are your biggest obstacle.

Become skilled.

Write it down and schedule it.

Choose to lose.

Have others hold you accountable.

Even though we can train ourselves to be more effective as leaders, it is a lifelong struggle that will never end completely. Self-management principles are strategies to help cultivate self-awareness, followed by ways to know when you might be winning some battles against self. These principles will show you practical steps to take toward being an effective leader, but the principles won't do the walking for you.

Principle 1   ***Realize that*** you ***are your biggest obstacle.***

In our culture of promoting strong self-esteem, thinking positive thoughts, and so on, being hard on yourself seems alien. But given our propensity to view ourselves more positively than we should and our tendency toward self-deception, self-awareness may be the most critical skill to master in becoming an effective leader. You must master yourself before you can remotely begin to influence others. This self-mastery is also critical to one of the primary methods of learning and teaching skills: modeling.

Leadership by example is not one form of leading—it is likely the only effective form. Being a leader, therefore, means devel-

Leadership by example is not one form of leading—it is likely the only effective form.

oping a mind-set that is strict and aggressive toward our-selves first, not primarily toward others. This perspective is not normal human behavior, and therefore we need con-stant structure and solicited feedback to avoid making the mistakes most managers make.

Principle 2 ⟩ **Become skilled.**

Part of managing yourself is recognizing your skill deficits and aggressively seeking to develop those skills. For instance, consider computer skills. Few would deny that one's ability to use a computer is absolutely critical in today's law enforcement culture. Word processing, email, and computer-assisted research are integral to every manager's daily routine. Some managers, especially those who are older, still resist technology, while others in the same age category learn these skills because they know computer proficiency is an important part of their job.

Another example of emerging skills is the ability to speak another language. If you work in a community with a large Hispanic and Latino representation, you can either wait for all new immigrants to learn English, or you can learn Spanish. Leaders always assume that learning is a lifelong experience—you have to acquire new skills to be effective. Many managers (especially evil managers) are threatened by these new demands and resist adaptation and learning.

A useful word picture was given to me years ago: Being effective is real-izing that the "Swiss army knife" we carry at work must become more complex and multifaceted in the fastest changing society in his-tory. We must constantly add new blades to our skills to be competent in today's culture.

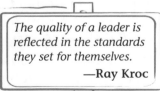

The quality of a leader is reflected in the standards they set for themselves.

—**Ray Kroc**

It should be obvious, however, that technical skills are not the most critical to the law enforcement manager. Given that intrapersonal and interpersonal skills are the keys to successful leadership—and the areas where skills deficits are likely to damage us most severely—we must focus on developing these skills. Since most of us have not had good modeling in these skill areas at work or at home, they may be difficult to learn. Obviously, the question becomes, how do we become skilled in the complex dimensions of human behavior and interaction? If our parents did not communicate well and most of our managers at work failed to demonstrate good communication, what are some methods we can use to overcome these skill deficits in our own lives? Disagreeing with the way our parents and managers communicated is not the answer. One of the most powerful principles I have learned from one of my mentors is that "you cannot change a behavior unless you replace it with another behavior." What are the methods we can use to make us more skilled in replacement behaviors?

Ideally, you can take a course in communication skills. If you can find a good one, by all means attend it. I warn you, however, that most communications courses are not that effective in teaching this critical leadership skill. Why? Most courses are not skills-based programs but primarily focus on lecture and discussion. Communication and listening are skills-based behaviors and can only be learned through "tell, see, do" methods of instruction. Can you imagine attending a firearms course or pursuit driving course that was entirely classroom lecture? A communications course that is lecture based will generally be ineffective. If you decide to attend a course, find one with a hands-on, skill-based training format.

Another way to learn communication is to *observe and learn from others*—both positive and negative communicators. Since much of our learning is based on modeling and visual recognition, this method may be better than a course for learning this skill, or it will at least complement a course on communication. Better yet, ask a manager who is a good communicator to teach you his or her skills. This is especially helpful if you are allowed to be with the person as he or she actually practices these skills in everyday events, such as confronting a problem employee. This method of learning skills through mentoring has been very effective in teaching police officers and deputies through Field Training Officer (FTO) programs. Yet another way to improve your interpersonal skills is to ask others to provide you feedback. How do you verbally and nonverbally relate to others, when communicating as well as when listening? Whatever methods or combination of methods you employ, remember that these are skills you must *repeatedly practice and master.*

Practicing Communication Skills

A friend told me that in his early years of marriage, he had a difficult time not being negative and demanding of his wife when he called her while out of town on business. He added that what was so frustrating was that he genuinely loved and appreciated his wife and would have all sorts of positive thoughts about her while he was out of town. When she answered the phone, however, he found himself focusing on criticism and having a domineering attitude. His positive thoughts were not matched by his skills of delivery. Why? He believed that he acted as he did on the telephone (and in person) with his spouse because he was mirroring how his father communicated. He added that even though he never agreed with the way his father talked to his mother, he was obviously modeling it in his own life. Given that this man has a great relationship with his wife today and communicates with her better than most of us do with our spouses, I was intrigued by how he had learned to master this skill.

He told me that he had trained himself to learn new skills to replace those he had been brought up with. How? By scripting his thoughts on paper before he called home or talked in person with his wife, he taught himself how to say what he really wanted to say. As strange as it may sound, he would write out things to ask his wife about as well as compliments that he sincerely believed. Once she answered the phone, he would use these written comments to make sure he did not resort to his naturally critical tone. At first, it was obviously unnatural and forced, but he eventually taught himself to share his good thoughts rather than focus on criticism. Though his wife likely realized that his early attempts were scripted and forced, she was probably so impressed by his intentions to be more positive that she forgave his awkwardness. After he told me this amazing story, I asked him if he still scripted his conversations. He replied that he did not because he had become proficient in this area—but it had taken many years to master this skill.

Can you use this method to learn work-related skills? Of course! *You already have.* We all used this method to learn skills as police officers. We had to read the Miranda Warning when we were rookies, but later we could recite it from memory. We know from experience that this method works, so why not try it to learn new leadership skills?

Principle 3   **Write it down and schedule it or you won't do it.** Remember Warning 2: The road to hell is paved with good intentions. Most managers intuitively think about ways to be effective as leaders—they just don't follow through. Leaders understand this tendency to forget to follow through, so they consistently *write down and schedule their good thoughts* to make sure these thoughts turn into actions. In today's busy and demanding work and home environments, leaders learn not to trust their memories or their feelings—they put structure to thoughts and emotions. In the words of one seminar participant's Marine "gunny" sergeant, "A short pencil is always better than a long memory."

We all need a method for immediately recording our good thoughts so that we will be reminded to do them later. Whether you use a simple pad and pencil, a tape recorder, or a handheld computerized organizer, choose a system you can always have with you to capture the many good and often thoughtful ideas that will make you an effective leader. One police manager who always comes up with these ideas on the way home from work developed a method of calling his office telephone and leaving himself a voicemail message that he would then transcribe onto a to-do list the next time he was at work. I promise you that if you begin to diligently practice writing down and then following through, you will be much more effective as a leader. You will also find out that when you follow through on these written reminders, most recipients of your efforts will remark that you are the only one who seemed to care enough to call or visit them at the hospital. Remember, however, that what this person said is not true—many people cared; *they just forgot to write it down.*

Scheduling specific times to follow through on what we know we should do is also an important intrapersonal skill. As earlier chapters describe, most managers agree that spending time with personnel is critical to being a leader, yet most of these managers never actually show up. Because they wait for it to be convenient or spontaneous, they do not act on their belief systems. The only way to succeed in this powerful form of showing others that you want to spend time with them is to schedule specific times in your work week for this positive contact with all subordinates. You must set appointments to practice leadership behaviors. This is exactly the same principle as scheduling specific times to spend with your children each week, but applied to the work environment.

> *You must set appointments to practice leadership behaviors.*

Principle 4 ▷ **Choose to lose—discipline yourself.**

All these principles require disciplining yourself to do things even when you don't feel like doing them. Someone asked me if I thought leaders were unselfish. I replied that I agreed with Lincoln's observation that *leaders are normal, selfish individuals who force themselves to do unselfish things.* The rule of thumb is that if you do what you feel like, you will be ineffective. If you force yourself to do what you know is the right thing to do, even when you are tired, you will be effective. As you can see, being a leader is basically a moment-by-moment struggle between your "bad" nature and your "good" nature to do what you know you should do.

Self-Sacrifice

A police chief told me about a time when new cars were delivered to his agency and he saw one that he really wanted to have. He was torn between doing what he wanted (to have the car for himself) or giving the car to an officer in his agency who really needed the vehicle. He eventually gave the car to the officer whose vehicle had the most mileage, "but," he added, with a sly grin, "I didn't want to." I told him that was all right; he had demonstrated the real struggle that all leaders go through every day. He added that on the day he gave the vehicle to the officer, he felt a great sense of satisfaction for going against his own selfish wishes.

He understood the primary motivation of a leader—to master oneself. When all is said and done, leaders are individuals who choose to lose yet ultimately win in their quest to be leaders.

Principle 5 ▷ **Have others hold you accountable.**

The final principle of self-management reinforces the other principles. Since self-discipline is not easily (if ever) accomplished, we need to use *positive and solicited peer pressure and accountability* to give us the courage to do the right thing. As discussed in the previous chapter, we always tend to be more disciplined when we have to face consequences if we do not perform to standards. We are also social creatures who tend to be self-deceived. Combine these weaknesses with the fact that we will be criticized for trying to implement leadership strategies, we had better ask others to help us in this extremely difficult endeavor. There are several forms this valuable form of support can take.

First, you can use the practice of *asking others to hold you accountable* for improving specific areas of weakness and following through on proactive strategies. Solomon expresses this principle clearly in Proverbs 27:17 (NASB):

> *"Iron sharpens iron, so one man sharpens another."*

Basically, to implement this principle in becoming a leader, you make a *written* list of several specific behaviors you want to see changed or reinforced, then give this list to two or more of your colleagues and ask them to hold you accountable. I believe you must have at least two people do this because it may be too difficult for one person to do this alone. In my experience, one person usually wimps out when faced with this task. Ask these people to meet at specified times (such as once a week) to go over the list with you and ask how you have done. If you have done something incorrectly—let's say, you offended a person—they should also encourage you to apologize to this person within a specified period. They will usually offer suggestions on how to master skills (or strengthen weaknesses). To make this procedure even more effective, have them give you lists of their weaknesses and goals for you to help them with as well. This mutual accountability is a more accurate and healthy way of implementing the "iron sharpens iron" principle.

Another version of this strategy is to *meet collectively with the individuals you supervise* and voice your concerns about your weaknesses and your attempts to be more proactive, asking them to provide you with feedback (individually or as a group) on how you are doing. Remind them that you have given them permission to confront you and to make recommendations. As an example, tell them that if they feel you have made a knee-jerk decision, they must come to you and ask you to explain your actions. If you sit in your office too much during the week, give them a deadline of a certain day to come to your office and remind you that you need to come out and mingle with the troops. It should be obvious that this method pressures them to offer constructive criticism rather than slander you behind your back. This is also an excellent way to mentor subordinates on leadership principles. This version of "iron sharpens iron" is best reserved for situations in which you know your team fairly well. If you tried this in a new assignment or group, it would probably not be successful.

Another version of accountability is the *use of evaluations and surveys* to solicit written responses from your team to specific leadership behaviors you are trying to model. I have always thought it impractical that sergeants are evaluated only by lieutenants or captains (who often rarely see them) and not by their subordinates. As a university professor and as a law enforcement trainer, I was usually evaluated by students—and rightfully so. Not only are students (and subordinates) more accurate evaluators of your performance than your superiors are, this feedback also accomplishes two other important goals. First, when you know that your subordinates are all going to evaluate you at some point, you tend to discipline yourself to be more responsive to their needs. If you know you will pay consequences for not listening, you are more likely to discipline yourself to listen and pay attention. Conversely, if you know that your superiors will evaluate you and that they rarely see you interacting with employees, there is minimal pressure to be proactive with your subordinates. Second, legitimate forms of critique and evaluation usually

> Very few of the great leaders ever get through their careers without failing, sometimes dramatically.
>
> —Philip Crosby

minimize rumors, gossip, and slander, which are always destructive to the interpersonal environment. I have also found that people are more gracious and forgiving when *legitimate* forms of feedback are available. Basically, there are few drawbacks to having *360 evaluations* done on all supervisors and managers. Comprehensive and all-inclusive evaluations just make more sense in building accountability and feedback.

Guidelines for Effective Evaluations

For those who have never seen or used subordinate evaluations, I have provided a draft of one on page 147. Whether you use this model or create your own, keep in mind a few guidelines.

1. Generally, evaluations must be written *anonymously* if they are to be effective. Most people are afraid of retaliation and will not fill out these forms honestly if they think they will be punished for doing so. For a similar reason, if the group being surveyed is very small, subordinate evaluations are limited in accuracy because there is no safety in numbers.

2. Interpret the responses to surveys by disregarding the *numerical* data associated with the highest and lowest scores. This helps prevent the problem employee who just got disciplined as well as the sergeant's buddy from influencing the scores too greatly.

3. *All* supervisors and managers should be evaluated for the system to be fair. For instance, it is not equitable for captains and majors to ask their lieutenants and sergeants to be evaluated if they are not evaluated by all subordinates as well.

4. *Follow through* on the results. Having employees fill out these forms is worthless if

you do not act on what they reflect. If managers who score low on these forms are not confronted and counseled to improve, the employees will see that the forms serve no purpose. Similarly, managers who score high on these forms should be affirmed and rewarded for their leadership skills.

An agency that uses one of the best-constructed evaluation forms I have ever seen does not use the data for counseling or promotional purposes. They just give the results to the evaluated manager as a form of feedback that the manager can choose to ignore. Therefore, the lowest-rated manager in this agency can be promoted even though his or her subordinates believe the person is a terrible manager. You can imagine what the rank and file think about this evaluation process.

Managing Yourself Now and in the Future

Leadership begins with learning how to bring yourself under control, not with how to make people do what you want them to do. Given that we tend to be self-deceived and defensive, how do we know that we are developing this self-mastery and not just fooling ourselves? The first litmus test is whether we are *acting* on some of the recommendations made about writing things down, "iron on iron" strategies, and other self-management techniques. The Action Items on page 74 will help you get started.

Another way to know that you are on the road to self-mastery is when you (and others) notice the following changes in your perspectives and attitudes. Foremost will be a change in *your perspective about yourself.* I think it is impossible to be even remotely successful in bringing yourself under control if you are egotistical. Facing yourself and your daily failures to follow through will not allow you to think that you are doing a great job as a leader. I have always found true leaders to be humble—they know themselves and their struggles too well to have an inflated view of themselves.

I think you will also notice a change in *your attitude toward others*. I don't believe there is any way to be working at self-mastery and be overly impatient or critical of other people. Managers who are genuinely seeking to control their temper will not overreact to others' outbursts of anger. Trying to do the right thing yourself always makes you more empathetic of others' weaknesses. One of the finest leaders I have ever known had to discipline me one time. His comments were powerful. He told me that I was wrong in my actions, but that he had often done the same thing in the past. He added that he knew I would improve in this area and that if he had not cared for me, he would not have confronted me. Whoa! Never had discipline affected me so dramatically. Struggling with yourself always makes you merciful to others when they make mistakes. Ineffective managers, however, are extremely focused on and often intolerant of others' weaknesses while being self-deceived about their own faults.

I warn you that the next chapters include some redundancy and repetition of the ideas in this chapter. Being an effective communicator (chapter 6), motivator and disciplinarian (chapter 7), and parent or spouse (chapter 8) will require you to write down, schedule, and have others make you learn and practice skills. Leadership by example is ultimately the only way to communicate, motivate, confront, and be successful in any environment. Failure to realize this will always lead us to be mediocre and ineffective leaders.

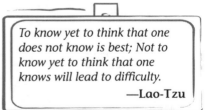

> To know yet to think that one does not know is best; Not to know yet to think that one knows will lead to difficulty.
>
> —Lao-Tzu

Action Items

1. List at least *four proactive things* you could do that would make you a more effective leader.

   _____

   _____

   _____

   _____

2. List at least *three weaknesses* you have that reduce your effectiveness as a leader.

   _____

   _____

   _____

3. Using your responses to (1) and (2), make a *list of behaviors* you want others to hold you accountable for.

   _____

   _____

   _____

   _____

   _____

   _____

4. Write the names of two or three people you
   would pick to hold you accountable. Who
   will be your iron men or women?

   _____

   _____

   _____

5. Pick one of the strategies of accountability
   discussed in this chapter (see pages 68–72),
   write it down here, and give it a try.

   _____

   _____

   _____

   _____

   _____

   _____

   _____

   _____

Developing Interpersonal Skills

Now that you have begun practicing the critical skill of managing yourself, you are ready to learn the skill of communicating in the law enforcement culture. In other words, once you have begun to demonstrate some self-mastery, you will be prepared to invade the lives of others. I cannot overemphasize, however, that if you are not actively learning to manage yourself, none of the suggestions in this chapter will work. If you are self-deceived, self-centered, and failing to follow through on your good intentions, you will probably fail at being an effective communicator. If your life is not matching your words, you have nothing to say to others. This is especially true with law enforcement officers,

> *If your life is not matching your words, you have nothing to say to others.*

who are extremely skilled at reading people and will easily identify behaviors that are fake, self-serving, or insincere.

Conversely, if you are a great person who masters nearly every principle of self-management, yet you never come out of your office, you will fail to affect the lives of others. I have known many fine men and women who possessed tremendous integrity and dedication to the profession and to their personnel yet failed to affect their agencies because they spent too much time on the administrative aspects of their jobs and did not communicate with personnel in the agency.

Law enforcement personnel are generally suspicious of and negative toward managers, so they must get to know you personally if you are to build their trust in you. We all trust people we know and distrust those we don't know. To build this trust, you need an *engagement strategy* and the *necessary communication skills* to make this strategy work.

The Rules of Engagement

You must invade the culture to win others, and to do this requires an engagement strategy. One of the most critical skills of leadership is developing and maintaining the mind-set that consistently engaging others is important. Being effective as a leader involves building others' trust in you, and you cannot build this trust without knowing those you lead and letting them get to know you in return. A leader understands that he or she can accomplish this task only through proactive and consistent communication, which means cultivating various communication strategies, planned and spontaneous.

When discussing their communication with employees, many law enforcement managers and executives have assured me that they have an open door policy, but having an open door policy is not what I am talking about! I have never known of an open door policy that actually worked, and for obvious reasons. First, it violates the chain of command, alienating the supervisors and managers between you and subordinates. Knowing this, most employees are understandably reluctant to incur the wrath of their sergeants and lieutenants by coming to your office, and thus the only people who seem to take advantage of an open door policy are chronic whiners and complainers. Second, coming to your office is intimidating and cultivates a perception of a citizen requesting an audience with the

> Leadership is a two-way street, loyalty up and loyalty down. Respect for one's superiors; care for one's crew.
>
> —**Grace Murray Hopper**

king. Whenever I invited in an employee passing by my office door, he or she was always uncomfortable in the alien environment of a manager's office (which is often associated with punishment and discipline). You should always be willing to talk to employees who come to your office, of course, but you must learn to focus on *going into their environment* if you are to be a leader. This *invasion* requires understanding the characteristics of proactive communication.

Proactive communication characteristics

First, proactive communication occurs in *your subordinates' workspace and environment* and in contact that is *nonconfrontational*. By going to their assignments and work areas, you show respect for their positions in the organization. By making the effort to go to them, you minimize the impression that you take yourself or your position too seriously. Personnel are also naturally more comfortable in their own environment.

Second, proactive communication means deliberately communicating when there is *not* a problem. Evil and ineffective managers generally talk to a person only when they are upset about something. This reactive and negative communication alienates employees and makes them associate management contacts with discipline and problems. If they see you coming, someone must be in trouble. Leaders must counteract this perception by building rapport with staff through nonadversarial contact.

> *Meetings are highly overrated as a way to build commitment;* it is in individual conversations that you earn the right to lead others.

Third, proactive communication requires winning people over *individually*. Understand that if you forget someone, you will not win that person. Meetings are highly overrated as a way to build commitment; *it is in individual conversations that you earn the right to lead others.* If you leave out individuals or certain categories of employees, you will fail to influence them as a leader.

Communicate with Every Individual

I know a police chief who did an excellent job building commitment among the rank and file police officers of his agency through his regular practice of talking with the officers. If while driving home he observed an officer on a traffic stop, he would often stop and make sure he or she was all right. The officers were always impressed by this spontaneous and frequent show of concern and cama- raderie. Unfortunately, this same chief never practiced this proactive contact with civilian personnel in the agency. He rarely went into the communications center or records division or other areas of the agency primarily staffed by civilian workers. As a result, civilian staff members were generally not committed to him and resented his exclusion of them in his habit of informal employee contacts. His actions implied favoritism toward sworn personnel that undermined his effectiveness as a police chief with a criti- cal component of the organization.

Proactive communication scenarios

Now that you understand the characteristics of proactive communication, how do you structure these contacts? Several scenarios are effective for building commitment and trust with employees. Foremost is "management by walking around" (MBWA)—wandering around and talking to employees. MBWA in its purest form occurs when leaders schedule specific times during the week to engage employ- ees under their command. Most chiefs who practice MBWA apply it only with those who work during regular business hours and in the immediate vicinity of the chief's office. In most law enforcement agencies of any size, personnel on the late night and early morning shifts have never seen a mem- ber of the command staff. Leaders, however, practice MBWA with *all* employees on *all* shifts and in locations that are not in the immediate vicinity. I can assure you that if you never spend time with employees who work from 11:00 P.M. to 7:00 A.M., this group will never trust you or be committed to you as a leader.

Other important opportunities for communication are *impromptu encounters* with employees. Riding on the elevator, buying a soda in the break room, and other unplanned encounters are always excellent times to engage staff positively. Because the encounters are not planned, employees usually deem them safe, so taking advantage of these opportunities is a powerful way to get to know employees and help them get to know you.

Impromptu Communication

A very effective police chief of a large agency told me that he always makes sure he is ready to communicate with employees he encounters at the gasoline pumps while he is refueling his car. He told me that some of his most rewarding and pleasant encounters with employees have been while leaning up against their cars and talking to them while the vehicles were fueling. Given the size of the agency, he generally does not know the people by name, but he always introduces himself and asks about them. Though the employees always appear uncomfortable in the beginning, the chief will usually see a much more relaxed and positive demeanor by the end of this five-minute encounter.

Though I started this section criticizing open door policies, another important opportunity for communication is *when an employee comes to your office*. Always make sure that you stop what you are doing and verbally and nonverbally pay attention to the employee. If you are busy on a critical task, explain this and ask for a few minutes to finish the task or ask the person to come back at a specified time; he or she will normally understand. As with all communication, your nonverbal behavior will be critical to your ability to demonstrate that you care about what the employee is saying. The only exception to being willing to engage employees who come to your office should be made with those individuals who wander in and out of your office on an ongoing basis wanting to chit-chat or complain. It is important not to let these people interrupt your workday. Cutting short their ramblings or asking them to come back another time is often essential in getting your work done. This habit of theirs should also encourage you to leave your office and practice MBWA!

Another excellent method for building trust with employees is to *structure a set of interviews* with all employees to identify problems and issues within the organization. This technique is especially beneficial if you are taking over a new position in an agency because it accomplishes two important needs for you with an unfamiliar group of people. First, it enables you to identify issues that you will have to address in your new assignment. Second, it is an excellent method of breaking the ice with staff who do not know you. It should be obvious, however, that you will need to respond to the problems and issues they reveal in the interviews once you have concluded your study.

> Remember that it is far better to follow well than to lead indifferently.
>
> —John G. Vance

The final communication scenario, and likely one of the most powerful, is the *special issue situation*. These situations are the very positive or very negative times in an employee's life, such as a promotion or a commendable act, or illness, injury, or loss of a family member. Communicating with others at the extreme high and low points of their lives may be one of the most important times to make sure you pay attention. If you do not, employees may see you as indifferent or uncaring.

Speak Now or Forever Hold the Pieces

A police chief in the suburbs of Atlanta learned the hard way not to take for granted the importance of communicating with employees during their low points. A co-worker who had been one of his closest friends and most staunch supporters in the agency had a serious medical condition that required her to be admitted to the hospital for a week or so. Though this chief constantly thought about calling her or going by the hospital, his schedule was unbelievably hectic, and he failed to carve out the time for a telephone call or a visit.

When the employee returned to work, her attitude had completely changed, and she became an adversary to the point of eventually suing the chief in federal court on a relatively minor issue. This chief told me that he paid substantially for failing to communicate with her during a difficult time in her life. Failure to make a fifteen-minute visit to the hospital had resulted in resentment and misunderstandings that caused him many hours in depositions and in hearings. Though her case against him was not successful, the loss of the relationship with the employee and the time spent in litigation were serious blows to his ability to manage the agency effectively.

Effective telephone calls and written communication

This discussion of proactive communication has primarily focused on face-to-face contact with employees, but another tool of effective communication is proactive *telephone contact* with employees. As with face-to-face contact, telephone contact must focus on nonconfrontational communication and is especially beneficial in special issue scenarios. Some of the most powerful examples of leadership communication I have seen have been when a manager called an employee who had experienced a personal tragedy, an illness, or an on-the-job injury. Proactive telephone contacts can also be regarding positive events like promotion, exemplary work, or the birth of a child.

All these situations also apply to *written communication* such as emails, personal notes, and other proactive narratives, such as a letter or note to a staff member who has experienced any of the scenarios mentioned in the discussion of telephone calls. The communication must be personalized to a significant degree to be effective—an employee obviously would not appreciate or value a form letter. As mentioned earlier, you will often find that your telephone and written communications were the only contact employees received. Why? Because you wrote down and scheduled the contacts.

Write it down and schedule it or you won't do it

At the risk of being redundant, I must stress that if you don't write down and schedule your good thoughts, you *will* fail to communicate consistently with your employees. Today's management environment is too complex and demanding to trust communication to spontaneous good thoughts you will probably forget in five minutes. If you do not develop the habit of writing down reminders to call employees, or if you fail to schedule specific times to practice MBWA, you will not practice these valuable forms of communication. The following case studies of proactive and effective leaders illustrate practical ways to write down and schedule communication.

Ways to Schedule Communication

Example 1: A chief of a large agency has a practice of scheduling one day a week to spend time working with the operational and administrative components of his agency. He will normally begin this workday around noon and work until after midnight to ensure that he has contact with all three work shifts of patrol officers, detectives, and administrative personnel. His uniform patrol and detective commanders are still in operational control of their personnel, and the chief will primarily use this time for such tasks as backing up officers at calls or assisting detectives in serving a high-risk warrant. The chief always lets the responding officer or detective sergeant maintain control of the incident while he is basically available to help direct traffic at an accident or to help arrest a suspect. This chief also attempts to spend time in the administrative and support divisions of the agency—talking with the records clerk who works the 11 P.M. to 7 A.M. shift is also important. The chief attributes his success at implementing this strategy of communication by scheduling the day a week ahead of time and then notifying his shift supervisors of his plans. This notification then obligates him to follow through on the day he has selected.

Example 2: Another chief, also of a large agency, has multiple approaches to communicating proactively with employees. First, he is the one mentioned earlier as engaging employees while getting gasoline for his issued vehicle. He also schedules his attendance at roll calls for the various patrol shifts about once a month. An interesting tactic he uses is to have his administrative assistant randomly select four personnel from the agency every week and schedule a thirty-minute session with each of them in his office. These sessions are very informal and allow the employee to talk about anything he or she wishes to discuss. The chief says that he always asks the employees at the conclusion of the meetings if they think the session is a waste of time, and they always enthusiastically reply that they do not and that they enjoyed the time with him.

Example 3: Every Monday morning, a police department manager always writes down the names of each employee he supervises on his weekly to-do list. This written list of a dozen staff members is his checklist to ensure that he goes to their workspaces that week and communicates proactively. He cannot cross an employee name off the list until he has performed this task. This checklist has enabled him to make sure he communicates consistently with everyone under his command.

Example 4: A supervisor of a sheriff's department in Texas was always discouraged that once he showed up at work, others' demands on his time prevented him from having any proactive time with his seven or eight subordinates. To deal with this problem, he always stops at the desk of each staff member *before* he goes to his office first thing in the morning. This practice allows him to touch base with each employee *before* work issues take precedent. The brief encounters enable him not only to assure employees that he is thinking of them, but also to read the employees to see if they are upset or angry about something. If so, he can follow up with a longer appointment later in the day. He added that if he ever misses this practice of talking to them before he goes to his office (a rare occurrence), they always seem concerned that he did not spend time with them.

Engagement Skills

Now that you know *what* to do to communicate, you need to learn *how* to communicate. If you consistently schedule proactive communication opportunities with your staff but come across as bored or impatient, your time with employees will be ill spent. *Remember: most of us are not good communicators.* We have generally not had good role models in our family or at work who taught us how to listen and respond effectively to others. As police officers, we concentrated on gathering facts and data from strangers, a totally different scenario from routine communication with subordinates and staff. Most supervisors and managers we've encountered talked to us only in reactive scenarios, often with few or no listening skills. As a result, most of us are not skilled in communicating with or listening to others. These skills are obviously best learned in personal contact with others, through practice and being mentored, but what skills exactly do you need to learn? They fall into four major categories: oral communication skills, nonverbal communication skills, listening skills, and written communication skills.

Oral communication skills

Law enforcement officers tend to be effective at talking with others—they have to do it more often than people in most professions, often in stressful or unpleasant situations. Communicating with staff, however, is a different context in which a few guidelines are useful for communicating effectively.

First, if possible, *prepare* for in-person encounters, especially if they are emotionally charged, such as confronting a problem employee. Any or all of the following preparation strategies will increase your chances for successful oral communication:

* *Script* what you want to say to give yourself a framework to rely on. This process helps organize your thoughts and will also help keep the conversation on track if you or the person you are talking to wanders off the subject.

* *Discuss with another person* (preferably a skilled communicator) your plan of communication and ask for feedback. This person will either affirm your plan or offer advice and alternatives that may help you better communicate what you have to say.

* *Gather facts* about the person or the event before you attempt to talk about it. All of us have had the misfortune of watching a manager make a knee-jerk remark or decision before getting all the facts. If you plan to ask a subordinate why he or she was late to work, find out from other supervisors if this tardiness is chronic or highly unusual.

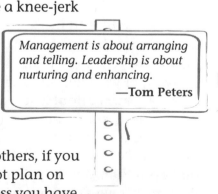

Management is about arranging and telling. Leadership is about nurturing and enhancing.

—Tom Peters

When it is time to talk to others, if you are emotional, you should not plan on attempting conversation unless you have no alternative. Many supervisors or managers (and agencies) would have saved themselves untold amounts of trouble if they would have learned not to talk to others while upset. If you must communicate with a person, and it is potentially emotional or confrontational, *always attempt to have someone else there with you.* Give this person permission ahead of time to stop you if you begin to lose it or say something inappropriate. Better yet, ask this person beforehand to take over the conversation if he or she senses that you are not handling the conversation appropriately. Another helpful hint when conversing with others is that if you don't know what to say (or want to say something that you should not), *keep quiet!* Inappropriate thoughts are always better than inappropriate words—and less legally and interpersonally damaging.

> If you don't know what to say (or want to say something that you should not), keep quiet! *Inappropriate thoughts are always better than inappropriate words—and less legally and interpersonally damaging.*

Of course, not all oral communication is potentially confrontational and negative, and many of these suggestions work for positive contacts as well. Scripting out your positive thoughts about people as well as finding out details of their commendable behavior will help you communicate more effectively. Listening more instead of dominating the conversation shows your willingness to hear about them and their issues. If you are attempting to talk proactively with employees and are not skilled at what to say, tell them you are not good at this! By explaining to them that you are trying to learn to be a better communicator and motivator, you show them your intent, and they will be more gracious and forgiving of your delivery methods.

Another important issue is the *use of jokes or sarcasm.* Law enforcement personnel are famous for their (often sick) senses of humor, especially in emotional situations. When in doubt, don't use it unless you really know the person well (and even then, sparingly). Some of the worst oral communication I have ever heard (or said) was in the context of making a joke. Once, I was introduced by a manager I knew well to his boss. I jokingly asked the manager if this was the boss with the drinking problem. The look on everyone's face made it clear the remark was not perceived as a joke. Yes, you guessed it—the boss was an alcoholic. As seen in this example, jokes and sarcasm are especially dangerous if you don't know the person. If you must use humor, self-depre-cating humor is usually safe—making fun of yourself is nor-mally the most risk-free way of interjecting humor into a situation.

Nonverbal communication skills

Many of us have heard the expression "it is not what you say, but how you say it." The phrase aptly summarizes the powerful impact of nonverbal behavior on the communica-tion process. Most of what we communicate is through our gestures, facial expressions, and other nonverbal behaviors. Law enforcement has long recognized the role of nonverbal communication in dealing with offenders. Many of the bet-ter interrogation skills focus on the interpretation of non-verbal cues, and most police officers have developed street skills of keying in on individuals who are acting strangely and suspiciously. Unfortunately, we have not often applied these operational perspectives to understanding com-munication in the orga-nizational culture. Let's briefly explore the vari-ous forms of nonverbal communication and their impact on communication.

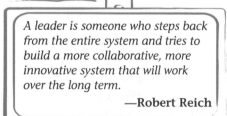

A leader is someone who steps back from the entire system and tries to build a more collaborative, more innovative system that will work over the long term.

—**Robert Reich**

Kinesics is a form of nonverbal behavior usually associated with *body language* and move-ment such as gestures and mannerisms. The most common form of kinesics behavior that we all recognize is the ten-dency of most individuals to cross their arms on their chest when they are uncomfortable and feel threatened by the contact or communication. Placing hands on your hips often indicates that you are going to lecture someone, and pointing your finger at someone when you are talking is always seen as confrontational. Nodding your head as someone is talking to you normally indicates that you understand and are encouraging the person to continue to talk. A person's posture can also provide evidence on such factors as fatigue or depression.

Proxemic behaviors are associated with the *use and impact of distance* in the communication process. The influence of space behavior is seen in the way we position ourselves when communicating with others. If you get out from behind your desk and sit directly across from someone you are conversing with, you will be perceived as listening. Leaning forward as the person is communicating may solidify this perception that you are listening. Think of how these proactive listening behaviors would benefit law enforcement officers and detectives when talking with victims and other citizens.

> *If you get out from behind your desk and sit directly across from someone you are conversing with, you will be perceived as listening.*

Paralanguage is the impact of *voice intonation* upon communication. The influence of tone, pitch, and speed are just a few of the factors that affect the meaning associated with our oral communication. All of us knew as children when our parent's tone of voice indicated we were in trouble. Paralanguage is obviously critical in telephone conversations, since it is the primary form of nonverbal communication we rely on when talking to someone not in our presence. If a manager talks quickly and abruptly on the telephone, it may indicate that he or she is in a hurry.

Facial expressions are also a form of nonverbal communication. The way we *use our eyes or contort our face or mouth* has a significant impact on what we are communicating. Most law enforcement personnel would agree that a lack of eye contact by a person indicates guilt just as rolling your eyes as someone is speaking indicates that you do not believe or trust what that person is telling you. Tightening your jaw or gritting your teeth is usually indicative of anger or frustration. When I was a child, this expression in my parents also meant that I was about to get a spanking or a tongue lashing!

Haptic behavior is associated with *touching* as a form of communication. *Appropriate* touching is one of the most powerful forms of nonverbal communication; it strongly indicates affection, support, or affirmation. Shaking hands or placing a hand on someone's shoulder while communicating can be strong and positive forms of communication—if the person who receives it trusts you and does not deem it as inappropriate. It should be obvious to anyone in law enforcement management today that inappropriate touching of members of the opposite sex, especially when combined with inappropriate verbal behavior, is evil conduct and an assault against someone, as well as fraught with legal issues. Confine most if not all haptic behavior to a handshake.

Chronemic behavior is the *influence of speed and time* on the communication process. The classic indicator that you are in a hurry is when you look at your watch. Most people would interpret this as your not having time to listen, which is obviously detrimental to the communication process. Other nonverbal behaviors of this type include becoming fidgety or continuing to walk away as someone is asking you a question. One of the more common forms of this behavior in law enforcement agencies is when a manager continues to work on a computer as you try to engage him or her in a conversation.

Appearance is another form of nonverbal behavior. Our *grooming and dress* have a significant impact on what we communicate to others. Any law enforcement officer who has worked narcotics will attest to the difference in how others perceive you when you change your grooming or dress. As managers, we can often interpret an individual's emotional health if we observe a negative change in an employee's personal appearance or that of his or her workspace or vehicle. Depression and stress are often first observed in the deterioration of a person's appearance or workspace.

It should be obvious to the law enforcement manager that nonverbal communication is critical to effective communication. What might not be so obvious, however, is *our tendency to always notice the nonverbal behaviors of others while failing to monitor our own*. Most managers are quick to point out that Captain Smith always types on his computer when you are trying to talk to him, but we all fail to notice when we do the same thing. Analyzing and monitoring your nonverbal behavior is essential to being an effective communicator.

Analyzing and monitoring your nonverbal behavior is essential to being an effective communicator.

Modifying Nonverbal Behavior

A police chief told me that he would subconsciously look at his watch when talking to employees until he was confronted by several subordinates and told that it gave the impression that he did not have time to listen. He said that he handled this situation by removing his watch when he got to the office. He then grinned and told me that he put a large clock on the wall behind the chair where employees sat so that he could look directly at them and yet see the time in his peripheral vision!

Listening skills

I read a survey years ago asking employees in the private sector to rate their supervisors' listening abilities. Only 10 percent of managers were perceived as good listeners; the majority of managers would not pay attention, would interrupt before a person was finished talking, or would do other things to indicate that they did not care to hear what the employee had to say. Anyone who has spent time in law enforcement would likely agree that this problem exists in our profession as well. The following are just a few of the suggestions from Sampson, Blakeman, and Carkhuff's *Social Intelligence Skills for Law Enforcement Supervisors/Managers*.

Nonverbal skills are of course critical to being a good listener. Good kinesics involve not crossing our arms and not slouching as people are trying to talk with us. Proxemic behaviors that pertain to effective listening include moving from behind our desks to sit across from people and leaning forward as they talk to us. This arranging and posturing technique positions us to hear better as well as to avoid the distractions on our desks. This position also communicates respect and enhances the comfort level of the person you are talking to. If your workspace does not permit this arrangement, then simply move your work aside on the desk and lean forward. Obviously, you should also watch your tone of voice and avoid rolling your eyes or glancing at your watch while listening and responding to someone. You can observe these behaviors in the other person to determine how well the conversation is going.

Oral communication as a listening skill is also important. Once someone has finished speaking, *paraphrase* briefly to show you understand what the person said. This serves two purposes. First, it shows that you are listening. Second, it allows the person to correct your misinterpretations, if any, of what he or she meant to convey. This *reflection* of others' communication is difficult to do and requires training and experience to master. If you are not skilled at this, avoid indicating emotions when paraphrasing. The most common error of this type is when a manager responds to a comment with a phrase like, "So you are angry about the promotional process?" The person may be just expressing concern about the process, so the manager would be incorrectly labeling the employee's emotions (which, interestingly enough, will make that person angry). The other oral communication skill in listening is often *not talking*. Do not interrupt people, and don't feel you have to have an answer to all their questions and concerns. All of us have had managers who will say whatever we want to hear, provide answers when they really don't know, or make promises without knowing if they will be able to deliver. "I don't know" may often be the most appropriate answer.

Another form of effective listening is making sure that we *follow through* on promises we made during the conversation.

Another form of effective listening is making sure that we follow through on promises we made during the conversation.

Saying "I will get back to you" about the topic and never following through will always negate the listening process. If employees ask you to check on something, make sure you do it. Conversely, if you ask them to do something, make sure you check with them later to find out if they followed through and to ask about the result. When you contact people later and ask the current status of the topic you discussed with them, you affirm that you were indeed listening to what they had to say. Don't forget, though, that if you do not write it down, you probably won't remember to do it.

Written communication skills

As a university graduate professor, I noticed that law enforcement personnel were always the best writers in the class. Given that law enforcement is one of the few professions that require writing and documenting information daily, however, it is no wonder they can write well. Law enforcement managers might take advantage of their existing skills to affect the organizational culture. Although writing should never be the *primary* form of communication to win commitment from employees, it is a significant way to reinforce your other communication strategies. As we shall see in the next chapter on motivation, law enforcement personnel also trust written communication more than they trust spoken communication.

I have found written communication to be beneficial when there is an emotional issue and when I am uncomfortable with my ability to convey the information through speech. Many law enforcement personnel find it difficult to tell people when they are proud of their actions or disappointed in their behaviors. As a result, we tend to avoid doing it, or we do it aloud in a confrontational or other inappropriate manner. A way to avoid this fight-or-flight response to communication is to write down your thoughts and either give them to the person involved or use them as a guide to your conversation. Always deliver negative information in person and avoid writing negative comments to others without telling them first.

One last observation about written communication: *always have others proofread your written communication.* We all naturally miss our own errors when we read our own writing, so give it to someone else to check (for typographical errors and grammatical mistakes but also for content). When the person finishes reading it, ask, "What do you think I was trying to communicate?" The response might surprise you, which means you might need to rewrite it, but it is best to find out if it is unclear *before* you disseminate it to everyone in the agency. If you have no one to proofread your written work and must do it yourself, read it out loud as you review it. This method will pick up more errors than just silently reading your own material. Don't rely on a computer program's spellcheck features to find all your mistakes, because they can still miss certain errors and even *recommend* incorrect spellings.

Why Others Should Proofread Your Written Material

A police chief in Texas shared a story with me that demonstrates the limitations of computerized spelling-correction systems. He had one of his employees who had a background in computer graphics make mouse pads with the police agency's name, mission statement, and telephone numbers for the various divisions and departments. The purpose of this project was to pass out the mouse pads to the business community as a form of advertisement and good will. After the chief gave me this information, he started laughing and shaking his head. He asked me if I knew anyone who might want a box of mouse pads with "Department of Pubic Safety" as the title! The employee said that he had put it through a spelling-correction program on the computer, but the chief reminded him that this program works only when the incorrect word is not a word as well.

Communicating effectively in the law enforcement culture requires various strategies and skills, but most important is that communication must be primarily *proactive*—you cannot wait for your subordinates to come to you. You must invade the lives of others if you are to be a leader. When you communicate, remember that what you say is not nearly as important as *how* you say it. Communication is an important issue because most, if not all, of us come into managerial roles without the prerequisite verbal, nonverbal, and listening skills. We simply are not good at talking with others, confronting them correctly, affirming them, or being able to listen to what they have to say. As self-management is the critical mind-set of the leader, communication is the critical skill that allows him or her to engage the culture effectively. Lack of the discipline and the skills to engage others effectively may be why most managers fail to be leaders.

> *Your best work and finest leadership moments as a law enforcement manager will likely be in those brief proactive encounters you have with staff.*

With this in mind, be encouraged that your best work and finest leadership moments as a law enforcement manager will likely be in those brief proactive encounters you have with staff. Those memoranda and policies you spent all your time on will likely never be read. It will always be in attending behaviors that you will have your most lasting impact.

Action Items

1. What supervisor or manager most positively affected you in your career? What attending behaviors did he or she demonstrate that built your commitment? Were these behaviors during MBWA, impromptu encounters, an office visit, or a special issue situation?

   _____

   _____

   _____

   _____

2. What supervisor or manager most negatively affected you in your career? What encounters or situations did this person handle inappropriately that made you not respect him or her?

   _____

   _____

   _____

   _____

3. What nonverbal behaviors do you observe in others that have a negative impact on their ability to communicate effectively with others?

   _____

   _____

   _____

   _____

4. What nonverbal behaviors do you sometimes exhibit that likely have a negative
impact on your ability to effectively
communicate with others? What proactive
strategies might you employ to minimize
these behaviors in your communication?

_____

_____

_____

_____

5. What special issue situation regarding
a subordinate or co-worker (such as a
promotion, injury, sickness, or loss of a
family member) do you need to pay
attention to through a personal visit,
telephone call, or written note?

_____

_____

_____

_____

6. Whom do you regard as the best communicator in your agency? What makes him
or her so effective? Consider asking that
person to mentor or train you in
communication skills.

_____

_____

_____

7. Develop a specific plan for practicing
MBWA with your staff and *write it down*.

_____

_____

_____

Developing Reinforcement Skills

Two divergent but critical skills of leadership pertain to motivation and accountability. These skills are complementary dimensions of leadership that one must use to manage the spirit of the organizational culture. One skill is the ability to encourage and reinforce good and exemplary performance, while the other is the ability to hold others accountable, using confrontation and discipline, when they exhibit marginal or problem behavior. *Few managers perform this dual role well. Most focus on one while neglecting the other.* Some managers focus on discipline and catching employees doing things wrong; they feel that it is not their job to encourage or recognize good behavior—employees are just doing what they get paid to do. Other managers will occasionally reward good behavior but refuse to confront marginal or problem behaviors. These one-sided approaches to leadership send a mixed message to employees, and neither tactic qualifies as leadership. A leader understands that he or she must use both approaches equally well; anything less sends a contradictory and confusing message on what one must do to survive and succeed in the law enforcement culture.

Three Types of Employees

To illuminate the motivational climate in the law enforcement agency, let's examine the three types of employees we usually encounter in our roles as supervisors and managers. The traditional and normal responses to these three types have created many of the morale problems and much of the frustration among personnel in most law enforcement agencies in this country. Understanding these types will also illuminate an "abnormal" response to the organizational culture—leadership that engages good behavior *and* confronts bad behavior.

The exemplary employee

All of us have had the opportunity and privilege at one time or another to supervise or work alongside an employee who requires little or no supervision. These individuals consistently perform their work at 100 percent, and their attitude and commitment are always exemplary. We enjoy working with and supervising these go-to employees because we can always depend on them, and they cause us no problems. Most supervisors and managers estimate that approximately 10 percent of employees fit this category.

The problem employee

At the other end of the spectrum is the problem employee. These individuals are also estimated to be about 10 percent of employees, yet they generate nearly all supervisory problems. They are often lazy; their attitude is usually terrible; and they seem to put tremendous effort into stirring up trouble, generating complaints with the public, and creating problems for supervisors and managers. If they apply for jobs with other agencies (which they rarely seem to do), we celebrate—and mislead the other agencies by giving them good recommendations. If terrorists took over an agency and stated that they intended to kill a hostage to make sure their demands were taken seriously, most employees and managers would immediately glance over at the problem employee as the most desirable candidate for execution.

exemplary employees
(10%)

reflective employees
(80%)

problem employees
(10%)

The reflective employee

The remaining 80 percent of employees are neither consistently exemplary nor consistently problematic. They do an adequate job and only occasionally create minor problems. They fall below the radar of most supervisors and managers because they don't draw attention to themselves—either positively or negatively. One of the primary reasons they do not attract attention is because most are hesitant, holding back, watching and reflecting; they appear to be reluctant to expend much emotional or physical energy on the operational mission. Why? They are confused about the organizational response to the other two types of employees.

Mishandling the Exemplary Employee

You would intuitively think that the work of exemplary employees would be applauded and rewarded in most (if not all) law enforcement agencies, but we do almost the opposite. The usual response to the best employees is to take advantage of them and overload them with tasks and assignments. Because they do such good work, we give every important and complex project to them, and they normally accept each one without complaint. As a result, they are tremendously overworked and overburdened. They work long hours and rarely get to take their meal break or go home on time.

> The usual response to the best employees is to take advantage of them and overload them with tasks and assignments.

As supervisors, we also respond to these best employees by appreciating them, but not by saying anything to them aloud, in writing, or in other tangible ways. We brag about them to other supervisors and *internally* appreciate them, but we don't brag to them. As we so often do in our personal and professional lives, we let our good thoughts convince us that we have articulated these beliefs to those about whom we have these positive feelings, and the exemplary employee performs his or her insurmountable workload with little or no affirmation from us as individual supervisors or from the agency culture as a whole. If you doubt this, I challenge you to look in the personnel record of the exemplary employee; you will find little documentation such as written commendations, awards, or other evidence that managers have gone out of their way to reward the employee's behavior.

The exemplary employee is not a person to be admired by the reflective employee. Though exemplary employees are usually respected by the rank and file, they are certainly not to be emulated. Who wants to get screwed over like the best employee? Combine this with the fact that the exemplary employee is underappreciated by the agency culture, and it's easy to see why the average employee sees little if any benefit in being highly committed to be the best police officer, deputy, or investigator in the agency. This is especially true when employees see how we respond to the problem employee.

Good Thoughts Alone Serve No Purpose

I was doing a training program in the Kansas City area and had just discussed the exemplary employee when during the break, I overheard three sergeants discussing among themselves how a particular officer was clearly the best police officer in their agency. They made glowing statements about his performance, attitude, and other traits. I interrupted and asked if any of the three of them had ever made these comments to the officer verbally. They looked at each other and then individually replied that they had not. I asked them what was the purpose of appreciating someone if the person didn't know he was appreciated? They agreed and stated that they intended to follow through by trying to encourage the employee in the future.

Mishandling the Problem Employee

Ask any law enforcement managers or executives what our response *should* be to the problem employee and they will likely respond with "discipline," "fire them," and other punitive verbiage. In reality, however, is that what really happens to problem employees? No! Most agencies respond to the problem employee by *ignoring the behavior.* If you want to be a problem employee in a law enforcement agency, there will not be any concerted or sustained effort to discipline you or even give you a below-average evaluation. If you don't believe this, examine the

Most agencies respond to the problem employee by ignoring the behavior.

personnel folder for the worst employee in the agency. What disciplinary documentation will you find? Little, if any! What type of evaluations has this employee been given? Probably average, or even above average. Every supervisor consistently takes the path of least resistance and doesn't hold the problem employee accountable for his or her lack of productivity, terrible attitude, and other negative behavior.

Another way we respond to problem employees is to refrain from giving them normal workloads or by putting them in assignments where they have little or no work to do. What a terrible punishment! Though they will get the same salary as the exemplary employees (which is grievous), if you think of it from an hourly wage standpoint, problem employees may be the highest paid individuals in the agency! Other tactics for dealing with problem employees are just as nonpunitive. We transfer them from one assignment to another, or send them to training to get them out of the office. Worst yet, we punish all employees for their behavior. If Officer Jones misuses the departmental telephone system to call his girlfriend in Seattle, what is the typical organizational response? Officer Jones is not confronted, but a new policy is developed for all employees. This policy now requires each employee to keep a log of every telephone call he or she makes, document the purpose and length of the call, and have a supervisor approve the call ahead of time. Many policies in the agency manual are likely in response to one employee doing something incorrectly.

> *If you can find a path with no obstacles, it probably doesn't lead anywhere.*
> —**Frank A. Clark**

Why don't managers confront problem employees? As mentioned earlier, not confronting bad behavior within the law enforcement culture is especially puzzling given that most supervisors spent their careers as police officers or deputies, confronting unwanted and criminal behavior on the streets. It would then seem logical that law enforcement supervisors would be naturally prone to confront the behavior of the problem employee—but they don't. Even the managers who concentrate on finding employees doing things wrong usually focus their micromanagement and punitive approach on those individuals who are *not* problem employees. You rarely see problem employees micromanaged, only individuals who do not require this type of close supervision.

Where Do Most Policies Come From?

After a discussion in class about the failure to confront problem employees except through policies applied to all employees, a sergeant brought me his agency policy manual. He opened the manual and started flipping through the pages and saying, "That's the Tom Wilson policy," "That's the Helen Smith policy," and other similar comments. He lamented that supervisors and managers have always had a practice of punishing everyone because of the acts of the problem employee. When I asked why he thought that was the case, he replied that it was because they did not have the courage to confront the problem employee and hid their cowardice behind shotgun policies that punished everyone.

Why don't police supervisors police the problem employee? A retired law enforcement manager told me that he believes this lack of confrontation is due to police work being concentrated on crisis management, not on problem solving. He elaborated that law enforcement contacts with problem behavior are normally confined to brief encounters with strangers, with the eventual result or success of this encounter never being known (or really cared about). Confronting personnel, however, is an encounter that the supervisor must live with because he or she will deal with that officer in the future. Police supervisors are more uncomfortable dealing with people they know than with strangers in the operational environment. As a result, supervisors avoid dealing with personnel issues.

One of the more serious and far-reaching results of not holding problem employees accountable is that they are often successful at getting promoted in the agency! Since their poor behavior and work have not been correctly documented, they are always eligible to compete for promotion and are likely to score well on written promotional examinations. Why? Problem employees have plenty of time to study while on duty (after all, we give them nothing to do), but more important, the material covered in the promotional exam is the problem employee's area of expertise. Most written examinations are based on policies and procedures, the content of which the problem employee has studied for years. In fact, he or she is probably the only one who has really read the policy manual. Who knows what the sick leave policy is for the agency? The employee who abuses sick leave. No wonder many problem employees are always at the top of the promotional list.

Who Knows the Policies and Procedures?

To prove my point about problem employees knowing the policies, try this little experiment. Go up to the worst employee you supervise and ask him or her what the sick leave policy specifies. The employee will say something like "Section 401.3 states that after three *consecutive* days of absence, you must go to Doctor Bill Smith of Citywide Medical Offices and get a written doctor's excuse." Why do problem employees know this policy? They know the policy because they have abused it for years. Ask the same question of the best employee you have. What will be his or her response?—"I don't know." Exemplary employees don't know the sick leave policy because they never take sick leave. I use this illustration because every written promotional exam I have ever seen has a test question on the sick leave policy.

Mishandling the Reflective Employee

This previous discussion is really not about how bad problem employees are but how our lack of accountability is interpreted by the majority of personnel—the reflective employees. As previously mentioned, our overwork and lack of appreciation of the exemplary employee has made reflective employees wary of being overly committed, and our failure to confront the problem employee confirms that suspicion. Furthermore, being a problem employee is not perceived as being that bad—these employees seem to do quite well in the organizational culture, especially when compared with exemplary employees. It is no wonder that the reflective employee is suspicious of the organization: managers talk about professionalism, dedication, and commitment, but they don't seem to reward it.

> *It is no wonder that the reflective employee is suspicious of the organization: managers talk about professionalism, dedication, and commitment, but they don't seem to reward it.*

How do reflective employees perceive the management response to their group? Our tendency to ignore them because they do not attract attention is especially tragic for several reasons. First, numerically they represent most employees. Second, if you think about it, this group is the most receptive to and affected by leadership. Why? Exemplary employees are usually self-directed, self-motivated, and self-disciplined, so supervisors and managers have little impact on their performance or motivation. Many problem employees (but not all) have endemic problems that go far beyond the workplace and cannot generally be changed to any significant degree. In addition, their behavior has been (and continues to be) reinforced by the agency culture, so they can simply transfer, rather than change their behavior, and work for any number of ineffective, normal managers. Reflective employees, however, have

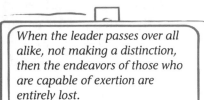

> *When the leader passes over all alike, not making a distinction, then the endeavors of those who are capable of exertion are entirely lost.*
>
> —Hitopadesa

been generally ignored by supervisors and managers, yet they truly respond to individual contacts by someone who pays attention to them. I believe that reflective employees are an untapped source for leadership strategies within the agency culture.

A rather provocative thought is that reflective employees may be the *best* source of effective supervisors and managers for the future. Though intuitively you would think exemplary employees would be the best pool for potential supervisors, they may not be. The best employees are independent and self-motivated and often find it difficult to make the jump from doing it themselves (independence) to having others do it (interdependence). Many agencies have found that promoting the best employees often results in a supervisor who is impatient with subordinates and prone to micromanage them in their duties. If not helped with this transition, exemplary employees may have difficulty giving up what has always been their strength—getting the job done themselves. Unless they are mentored and trained to make that jump from doing it to letting others do it, they can fail to be effective leaders.

Reflective employees, conversely, are often more people oriented and empathetic. After all, they have made their mistakes and been discouraged, so they better understand motivation and making mistakes—unlike their exemplary counterparts. Above all, reflective employees are usually watchers, observing and learning from what goes on in the agency. They tend to be emotionally smarter than exemplary employees, who are often too focused on operational tasks and too overworked to pay attention to what is going on in the agency culture and subcultures. We see this phenomenon in the development of effective coaches in professional sports. The best coaches are rarely the star players but are the competent players who did not always get to play. While they sat on the bench, they observed the strategies and the emotions associated with the game, which they later rely on as coaches.

The mishandling of exemplary and problem employees is a confirmation that leadership is abnormal behavior. No one seems to disagree with this synopsis of how the three types of employees are being mishandled in the agency, but no one seems to want to challenge it or try to change it either. This situation only underscores how difficult it is to be a leader in today's law enforcement agency. As a leader, you *will* encounter resistance if you attempt to deviate from the traditional approach to the three types of employees. Because a correct leadership approach to these issues is rare and does not come naturally, most of us need to learn specific strategies for dealing with all three types of employees. How does a leader respond to exemplary and problem behaviors? Through an effective use of both motivation and reinforcement.

> *It doesn't take a majority to make a rebellion; it takes only a few determined leaders and a sound cause.*
> —H. L. Mencken

Motivation and Reinforcement

Most experienced law enforcement personnel and managers would likely say that motivation is rarely used in the policing culture. Most in this profession have probably never been on the receiving end of encouragement for good work; nor have they seen it consistently applied to others in the agency. Why? Let's examine this failure from both *occupational* and *individual* perspectives.

Occupationally, as discussed in chapter 2, law enforcement personnel have been trained to ignore good behavior and concentrate on bad behavior. First, they have focused their operational observational skills on recognizing individuals who are doing something inappropriate or illegal. They will spend hours on patrol passing hundreds if not thousands of people, yet if the citizens are acting normally, police officers and deputies will really not pay attention to them. If someone starts acting abnormally, however, by doing something wrong or foolish, the cop's mental radar kicks in and he or she will usually engage that person. What makes us think this police officer or deputy will act any differently when promoted to sergeant? He or she will continue to focus on problem behaviors, not on commendable behaviors.

Another occupational experience that may be detrimental to one's ability to motivate others is more emotional. Law enforcement personnel usually develop emotional detachment in dealing with people and issues they encounter in police work. They have developed a response that is stoic and outwardly indifferent to the sadness and tragedy they witness daily. They often bring this stoicism home as well, as many families will attest. This is important to the skill of motivating employees because encouraging employees is to some degree an emotional transaction that is uncomfortable to many law enforcement personnel. It

> *It just feels strange to most supervisors and managers to say words of encouragement and affirmation.*

just feels strange to most supervisors and managers to say words of encouragement and affirmation. Combine this with the emphasis on recognizing only bad behavior and it is no wonder that most supervisors are not skilled at encouraging others.

From an *individual perspective*, law enforcement supervisors might not motivate others because of personal issues. A certain percentage of supervisors and managers are *self-centered and individualistic* in their approach to life; they are too concerned about their own careers and needs to care much about encouraging others. All of us have met evil managers (and some ineffective managers) who pay attention only when they will personally benefit from the person or situation. I have actually seen exemplary employee behaviors criticized by supervisors who felt threatened by the behaviors, which they might have perceived as giving the employees possible advantages in future promotions. Self-centered people will not genuinely encourage others, and they cannot be leaders.

Another person who will not motivate others is the supervisor or manager who is embittered toward the agency. Some veteran employees and managers resent their lack of advancement or some career disappointment or setback and have strong feelings of anger toward the agency. This resentment does not allow them to encourage employees for exemplary behavior—after all, the agency is out to screw everyone, so it really doesn't matter if you do a good job or not. This victim mentality will most likely preclude the

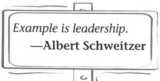

Example is leadership.
—Albert Schweitzer

cynical manager from ever motivating employees.

If you are not self-centered or embittered, it is still difficult to be a skilled motivator in the law enforcement culture. Most of us did not have these skills modeled to us in the past. Combine this with our tendency to be self-deceived by our good intentions and it is no wonder many of us are failing. We can intellectually agree with motivation and encouragement, but without seeing them modeled and practiced, it is difficult to implement them in our own lives. Without discipline, accountability, and training, being "brought up" in your career by supervisors who did not motivate you or others will often influence you to repeat their behavior. Our tendency to be deceived by our good thoughts makes us believe we have articulated our affirmations when we have not. Remember—good thoughts are worthless and serve no purpose. Motivation does not mean thinking positively about personnel; it means acting on the good thoughts most managers have. We can turn those goods thoughts into action from two perspectives: individual recognition and reinforcement that helps build group cohesion and belief systems.

> *Motivation does not mean thinking positively about personnel; it means acting on the good thoughts most managers have.*

Reinforcement to encourage stronger behavior in individuals
Many of us have heard of B.F. Skinner's theory of positive reinforcement. Basically, Skinner believed that if you positively recognize good behavior, it reinforces the behavior, and the individual will repeat it. We apply this theory in training the working dogs we use in law enforcement, such as patrol dogs as well as narcotics and bomb detection dogs. We also use the same methods in potty training our children. How can we apply this in the work environment?

Potty Training as Positive Reinforcement

Many managers who attend my training programs disagree that human beings require rewards and encouragement—it's a "bunch of psychobabble." They add that clear policies, punishment, and other similar strategies are the only way to get employees to work. I always ask them if this approach worked to toilet train their children. At first, they look puzzled, and then they begin to smile or laugh. Most of us potty trained our children with lots of verbal and tangible positive reinforcement, and it worked. As adults, we are no less susceptible to encouragement than we were when we were two years old.

Oral reinforcement. The simplest form of positive reinforcement is *oral*—simply telling people that they did a good job. If you look back on your own life, you will probably remember the best compliments you ever received as being brief but very powerful. Though often lasting ten seconds or less, being told that "you are an excellent police officer, one of the best I have seen in my career" or "I wish I had ten more employees just like you" is a brief event that you will remember for the rest of your life. If they are so simple, why don't we use oral compliments? I think that of all the forms of positive reinforcement, they are the most susceptible to being an emotional transaction, so we avoid them as supervisors. Law enforcement personnel are uncomfortable giving (and receiving) oral compliments, so we tend not to use them. If we do give them, we often make some humorous remark to make them more palatable. I have also found that because employees are distrustful of supervisors' intentions, they are more often suspicious of oral compliments than of other forms of reinforcement.

A potent variation on the oral compliment is the *second-hand compliment*. This form of compliment is especially valuable for middle managers. Basically, it begins either with overhearing a first-line supervisor brag about an employee or by asking supervisors who has done a commendable job among their staff. Once you have that information, you pass on the compliment to the employee; for example, "Sergeant Smith said you did an incredible job on the investigation, one of the best he has ever seen." Why is this type of compliment so effective? First, employees usually believe a secondhand compliment because the messenger (you) is not the source, so they do not perceive an agenda behind the compliment. Second, the supervisor was bragging about the employee without that employee present, which is more powerful than the average compliment. Yet another advantage of this type of compliment is that you are helping your supervisors by relaying information and encouragement they may not be skilled in delivering.

The Typical Cop Compliment

Because of the emotional nature of giving someone a compliment, law enforcement personnel usually have to interject sarcasm or other forms of humor to make the compliment easier to digest and to ensure that the hearer "doesn't take advantage of me." The typical cop compliment goes something like this: "You did a great job on that case. I was surprised and thought it was someone impersonating you or that you had a twin brother." Though injected with humor, it is still sincere, and most personnel perceive it as such.

Written reinforcement. A perhaps more effective and appropriate form of reinforcement for law enforcement is the *written compliment* or encouragement. Why? Written compliments eliminate many of the weaknesses of the spoken compliment, for both the sender and the receiver. As supervisors or managers in law enforcement, we are naturally more skilled at putting our thoughts in writing than in any other form. A sergeant who would be uncomfortable affirming a subordinate in person is usually excellent at writing these same thoughts. The written compliment is also not as emotional as the spoken one, so the supervisor will more likely use it. Employees are rarely suspicious of a written compliment. Why? Written documentation is perceived in the law enforcement profession as being proof, or evidence, so personnel logically trust written compliments more than spoken ones. Personnel generally trust written compliments also because the supervisor or manager took the time and effort to write them down. Other positive characteristics of written reinforcement include its capacity to be shared with others and its potential career-enhancing potential by being in the employee's personnel file. All these factors make the written compliment a valuable tool in the hands of the law enforcement leader.

> *Employees are rarely suspicious of a written compliment.*

Tangible reinforcement. A type of individual reinforcement that is fairly new to the law enforcement culture is the *tangible* form of reinforcement. This reward is normally something we can touch or feel, such as ribbons, medals, and other physical symbols of excellence. If you played high school or college football, you may have worn decals on your helmet to document unassisted tackles, touchdowns scored, and other acts of achievement. Anyone who served time in the military has been exposed to this type of reinforcement. Napoleon Bonaparte is reported to have remarked that "a man will not sell you his life, but he will give it to you for a piece of ribbon."

The most common form of tangible reinforcement we see in the law enforcement culture is the *ribbon and medal system*. This inexpensive system of recognizing good behavior is probably used by fewer than half of all agencies. If the system of selecting individuals for ribbons and medals is perceived as being fair, these items can be an excellent form of recognizing the better employees in the agency culture. The obvious limitation to the ribbon and medal system is that it is geared toward those employees who are in a uniformed position, so civilian personnel and investigators receive limited or no benefit from this type of recognition. With this in mind, let's examine some other forms of tangible reinforcement that can be used for all personnel.

The Power of Tangible Reinforcement

One of the best stories I have heard about the impact of tangible reinforcement in a law enforcement agency came from a police chief who was approached by the head of a pizza chain. This business leader offered to supply the police chief with magnetic pizza slices, four of which would form a pizza that was about two inches in diameter. The purpose of the program was to give the chief an opportunity to reward good behavior by passing out the magnetic pizza slices for commendable work. When an employee got four pizza slice magnets, he or she could go to the restaurant in this city and get a free pizza. During the first six months or so of the program, the chief handed out dozens of magnetic pizza slices—but no one redeemed them for pizzas! Since the pizza chain required that you turn in your magnetic pizza slices to get your pizza, employees refused to redeem them, preferring to keep the magnets on their file cabinets or refrigerators as symbols of their achievements.

The newest form of tangible reinforcement used by some law enforcement agencies is the *challenge coin*. These coins, also created first by the military, are normally somewhat larger than a fifty cent piece and have the departmental symbol and some type of statement or motto that denotes achievement or success—and they must be earned by the recipient. Though law enforcement personnel usually scoff at the coins as psychobabble when they are proposed, most agencies who use this system of reinforcement have found that personnel greatly appreciate them once the system is in place. Most of these coins have striking colors and engravings and are highly prized by personnel who receive them. They have become so popular among law enforcement agencies that display cases are now being marketed to enable employees to display them in their work area. The only downfall of these coins is that they are fairly expensive to have minted and produced, so many smaller agencies cannot afford them. Other forms of tangible reinforcement

can include such things as plaques, pens, and other, sometimes imaginative forms of reinforcement.

An Economical Alternative to Challenge Coins

A chief of a small agency (fewer than a dozen personnel)
told me that he had investigated the challenge coin but
found it too expensive for his agency budget. As an alternative, he went to a local bank once a month to get silver
dollars. Since these coins are rarely seen in everyday circu-
lation, he used them as reinforcement coins for agency
personnel. The employees enjoyed the symbol of recognition and would often display the coins on their desks or
constantly carry them in their pockets.

Reinforcement to build a stronger culture

Though most of us have heard about positive reinforcement
and its importance in building individual commitment, the
use of encouragement to build a stronger culture is much less
familiar to law enforcement managers. Researchers who
study organizations have recently promoted the idea that a
stronger motivation than individual recognition may be *the
motivation to be part of a mission or organization that we are
proud of*—we all want to believe that our job is important.
This concept is sometimes described as *dualism*, the idea that
all human beings have two
motivational needs. The first
need is to be recognized for our
individual achievements (positive reinforcement). The second
need is the need to be part of
something important. Basically, a higher form of motivation
is not to believe that our individual efforts are rewarded but
that we are part of a mission or group that is significant.

*A higher form of motivation is
not to believe that our individual
efforts are rewarded but that
we are part of a mission or
group that is significant.*

I cannot help but think of the United States Marine Corps
as an example of an organization that has mastered this
concept of dualism. Anyone who is now or has been a
Marine always talks with pride about being a Marine and
tends not to emphasize specific individual accomplishments.

Pride in being associated with and a member of the Marine Corps seems stronger than the Marine's need for positive reinforcement. The Marine Corps has accomplished the goal of creating dualism in a culture. Can we apply this concept to the law enforcement culture as well?

The Marine Corps and Dualism

The coordinator of personal security detail for the commandant of the United States Marine Corps told me that whenever the general was introduced at a press conference or briefing as the commandant of the Marine Corps, he would immediately clarify his perception of his position. He would tell the audience that he was actually "a Marine Corps rifleman currently assigned to the position of Marine Corps commandant." This individual was clearly more proud of his status as a Marine than of the stars on his shoulder epaulets.

You would think that as another warrior class culture, law enforcement could develop this "believing you are a part of something important" philosophy as the Marine Corps has. Unfortunately, we don't see that in most agencies. I have personally observed this strong culture in only a few agencies, such as the Royal Canadian Mounted Police and the Texas Rangers. Most dualism in law enforcement is probably in individual units or assignments like tactical squads or narcotics units. These assignments usually have a high level of camaraderie and group identity, and members normally resist being transferred from these units. Though this unit identity is commendable, it can sometimes have its downside if personnel develop cliques and a sense of being separate from the rest of the organizational culture. How does a leader use encouragement and motivation to develop

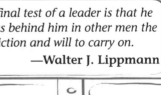

The final test of a leader is that he leaves behind him in other men the conviction and will to carry on.
—**Walter J. Lippmann**

dualism among his or her personnel?

Verbally, leaders shift their *encouragement* from "you did a good job" to "because of what you did, this happened." Consider, for example, the arrest of a drunk driver. Positive reinforcement would be telling the officer or deputy that he or she did a good job on paperwork and documentation of the arrest. Building a culture that believes in its mission, however, would mean telling the arresting officer or deputy that because he or she did the job, a family likely arrived safely at home instead of being hit by the drunk driver. You can see this approach would be extremely difficult for supervisors who have a hard time articulating encouragement at all, much less a more significant touchy feely remark. Most supervisors might be more comfortable using written letters or memos to convey this important belief system.

Some agencies have used the challenge coin system to build this type of belief in the group mission. Instead of rewarding personnel for individual achievement, managers give these coins to everyone in the agency. The purpose of this tangible reinforcement is to build a sense of membership in the agency or a belief about the mission. I have several coins of this nature, and they are very impressive. One has the names of every officer in the agency who has been killed in the line of duty as well as the motto, "One Team, One Family." Others have the agency core beliefs or other statements meant to foster a belief in the operational mission of law enforcement. Please note, however, that these coins will not affect a culture if the daily management philosophy violates the principles inscribed on the coins. Tangible reinforcement of this type is only a support system for valid leadership practices as discussed throughout this book.

> **Motivation Skills**
> Developing your skills as a motivator and encourager requires the same approach as other leadership skills.
>
> 1. *Write it down and schedule it.* Make sure you follow through on your good thoughts

about employees by having personal documentation and scheduling strategies that make you act on specific ideas for motivation and encouragement as well as thinking about them.

2. *Practice MBWA* so that you find out about the good things and the exemplary behavior of your employees. If you do not maintain ongoing contact with personnel, you will not know about their good work, nor will your affirmation mean much to them.

3. *Take care not to show favoritism* in your use of motivation and encouragement. I cannot emphasize too strongly that we all naturally show favoritism in our dealings with others—it is normal human behavior to do so. Unfortunately, there are few things that will damage your attempts at leadership more than showing favoritism to friends or favorite employees. In surveys that I conducted in eight law enforcement organizations, favoritism was ranked as the most common mistake by supervisors and managers. As a manager (and especially if you want to be a leader), you have lost the right to show any partiality in the way you treat others when it comes to rewards. This does not mean that you reward bad behavior as well as good; it means that when the circumstances are the same, you give your favorite employee no more affirmation than you give to one who has disappointed you in the past. Our tendency to show favoritism also underscores the criticality of MBWA; we have only partial and selective knowledge of commendable behavior among personnel if we sit in our offices too much.

The Other Side of Reinforcement—Holding Personnel Accountable

Accountability is critical to motivation and reinforcement because encouraging exemplary behavior yet failing to discourage (through discipline) behavior that is marginal or destructive is a contradictory approach to leadership that will always fail. There are many excellent books, articles, and courses on dealing with problem employees and the disciplinary process, so instead of a comprehensive examination of the topic, this section briefly covers some recommendations that relate to earlier discussions of leadership skills, communication, and why managers are failing.

First, keep in mind that *disciplining others is extremely difficult* to do. I just mentioned the voluminous amounts of material and courses on the topic, yet we know that discipline is rarely done. It is much easier to talk about that person than to talk to that person, so remember that you must *discipline yourself* to do what most other managers are not doing. The rest of the managers in your agency are not likely to applaud or reinforce your attempts to discipline problem employees. In fact, you must enter into the decision to discipline with the firm knowledge that others in the hierarchy may not support your efforts. If you correctly document, reprimand, progressively discipline, and do all the necessary steps, it is quite possible, if not probable, that someone above you or in a decision-making role (like a personnel board or city attorney) will not back your recommendation and will refuse to discipline the employee. Does that mean you wasted your time? No! As we have already discussed, a leader does the right thing even if it is not rewarded. So what is the benefit?

> *There is nothing more difficult to take in hand, more perilous to conduct or more uncertain in its success than to take the lead in the introduction of a new order of things.*
>
> —Niccolo Machiavelli

When you discipline marginal and problem behavior, you positively affect all three categories of employees. You reinforce the good work of exemplary employees by showing that those who fail to perform are being noticed and confronted. You also make a statement to the problem employees that they all will pay consequences for not doing their work or for exhibiting unwanted behavior. If your discipline of the problem employee is overturned, it still does not change the fact that you confronted the employee. As difficult as it is to confront others, it is twice as uncomfortable to be confronted. For the offending employee and other marginal performers, this discomfort alone may make them think twice before committing another infraction. A subordinate who does something inappropriate every week may limit that behavior to once or twice a month if he or she sees you taking accountability seriously. If the problem behavior is abuse of members of the public or agency personnel, potential victims may be minimized. Is that not a worthy goal even if your discipline is not supported by the ultimate decision makers?

Why We Should Hold People Accountable

A clinical psychologist who conducts fitness-for-duty examinations of law enforcement personnel sees one thing in common among cops he has examined. Other police officers and supervisors observed the cops abusing alcohol, having on-duty extramarital affairs, and participating in other destructive behaviors but never pulled them aside to warn them of the consequences of these actions. Because no one cared enough to hold them accountable, these officers continued in their behaviors, and many eventually lost their jobs. Certainly, some of these people would have disregarded their peers' or superiors' attempts to hold them accountable, but who will ever know?

The types of employees that will benefit most from your disciplinary efforts, even when these efforts are not supported, are reflective employees. This majority of employees will (often silently) applaud your efforts because they don't respect the problem employee. The problem employee causes them to do more than their share of the work and aggravates them with his or her constant whining and complaining (even though the reflective employees will often chime in). Plus, reflective employees will make mistakes, and your attempts at accountability will minimize the risk that they will do marginal work because they think no one cares about standards. *Most important, you are showing them how to be a leader.* When you discipline employees for marginal behaviors, you show future supervisors and managers how it is done, remedying the absence of appropriate modeling that most of us had earlier in our careers. When you discipline problem behaviors, you are mentoring the future leaders of the agency.

Two Types of Problem Employees

I have encountered two types of problem employees in my careers. The first type is the chronic, long-term problem employee that has had a consistently bad record since his or her graduation from the academy. My experience is that few of these people can be changed.

The second type is the one that was a reflective (or even an exemplary) employee earlier in his or her career. This second type may be redeemable, and one of your goals should be to talk to all such employees and find out what happened to cause their attitudes or performances to go south. Maybe an employee had a bad experience with a supervisor in the past and began to become cynical and resentful toward the agency. You may be able to win this person back if you offer him or her a chance, especially if you are a new supervisor. I have personally seen instances of two problem employees of this latter type turn around and become competent employees.

As always, you should *gather information* on the person and the incident *before* you confront someone. Disciplining another is so critical that you should never rush into the process or do it in a knee-jerk manner. Have your facts in order before you engage the employee. Next, *script* what to discuss in the meeting to keep you on track, and be sure to *take another supervisor or manager with you.* The presence of another person who is there to offer moral support (and intervention if necessary) will make you do a better job in the disciplinary process. From an appeals or grievance standpoint, having a witness to what was said in the encounter is also invaluable.

> *You have to lead people gently toward what they already know is right.*
>
> —**Philip Crosby**

Another important recommendation is to make sure you do not discipline someone for a mistake or error in judgment to the same degree you would do if the person knowingly and willingly violated a policy or procedure. Law enforcement is one of the most complex tasks in the world, and in each situation there is a strong probability of making a decision that may not work or that may result in letting our emotions get the best of us. I once worked for a great supervisor who often said, "The only people who don't make mistakes are those that don't do their jobs." There is a lot of truth in this statement. Make sure you don't derail the learning process that we all must go through by overreacting to mistakes and errors in judgment. In the same vein, always use a mentoring process by not only confronting the person who behaved inappropri-

> *Always use a mentoring process by not only confronting the person who behaved inappropriately, but also recommending a better way the situation could have been handled.*

ately, but also recommending a better way the situation could have been handled. This "here is what is wrong, and here is how it could have been done" approach is always more beneficial than just hammering away at what was done wrong.

In some ways, developing reinforcement skills is a synthesis of developing intrapersonal and interpersonal skills.

Motivating others and holding them accountable require following through in your communication with others to show that you are backing up the words of leadership with action. Communication without confirmation of and confrontation regarding behaviors will fail to affect the culture; instead, we can reinforce the culture by bringing leadership in action to the daily lives of the personnel we supervise.

Most agencies in law enforcement have plaques throughout their facilities verbalizing "core values," "agency philosophy," or similar statements about ideals and belief systems, but those displayed beliefs are mostly verbiage because the average law enforcement employee does not see them practiced daily. By engaging those around us, paying attention to both good and bad behavior in every employee, we bring reality to these values. We walk the talk when we practice leadership in its purest form by encouraging good work, confronting those with marginal and problem behaviors, and mentoring those who are struggling to choose between the two.

> Anybody who accepts mediocrity—in school, on the job, in life—is a person who compromises, and when the leader compromises, the whole organization compromises.
>
> —**Charles Knight**

Action Items

1. If you manage a group of personnel, where does each employee you supervise fit within the three types of employees? Write down the three types (see page 100) and list names next to each type.

   _____

   _____

   _____

2. Use a spoken, written, or other tangible form of reinforcement to tell exemplary employees that you labeled them as exemplary. Articulate to them why you feel that they are the best employees in the agency.

   _____

   _____

   _____

   _____

3. What are the best spoken, written, and tangible forms of encouragement you have been given?

   _____

   _____

   _____

   _____

4. In chapter 3, you were asked to describe the best leaders you have been exposed to in your professional and personal life. Write each one of them a brief note telling them that you selected them as such and share the characteristics you listed to describe why. If one of the

individuals is deceased, consider writing the note to his or her family.

_____
_____
_____
_____

5. What commendable act of one of your subordinates have you failed to recognize? Rectify that issue in the next ten days.

_____
_____
_____
_____

6. What marginal or problem behavior do you need to confront? Develop a strategy, research the person and incident, and plan on meeting with the individual in the next ten days.

_____
_____
_____
_____

7. If you have developed an accountability list and "iron men" and "iron women" to make sure that you follow through (see page 69), add both motivation and accountability issues to your list.

_____
_____
_____
_____

Managing Your Personal Life

8

Physical Fitness

Emotional Fitness

Family Relationships

What percentage of law enforcement managers consistently demonstrate leadership in the organizational culture? As you might remember, most law enforcement personnel I have polled estimate around 10 percent, meaning that most managers fail to be effective. What if we adapted that question to our personal lives? What percentage of the people you know are effective spouses and parents, people who have been successful in building great marriages and families? When I ask that question in training programs, the answers generally mirror those associated with leadership in the workplace—around 10 percent. This scarcity of individuals who are effective in their personal relationships might also be observed in other areas, such as finances and fitness.

The bottom line appears to be that most of us do not demonstrate success in our relationships or in the ways we handle our money or take care of ourselves.

Fortunately, we can apply the same principles of leadership we are learning to practice in the workplace to the effective management of our personal lives. Why is this important to do? Though intuitively we all believe our relationships, finances, and fitness are important, elaborating on how and

> *Fortunately, we can apply the same principles of leadership we are learning to practice in the workplace to the effective management of our personal lives.*

why managing our personal lives is essential will underscore just how critical these areas are to all facets of our lives. First, our success or failure in our personal lives affects our ability to be effective in the workplace. If you have been a manager in a law enforcement agency, you know how problems in personal finances and relationships always seem to influence behavior on the job. It is unrealistic to assume that a police officer who is having serious problems with debt or is going through a difficult divorce will not be affected by these situations while in the workplace.

Another reason that success in our personal lives is critical is related to the simple fact that, from a perspective of time, we are all engaged in a life that is primarily not associated with work issues. Not only do we spend most of our time away from the workplace, most of us will retire and face a life that is not related to our law enforcement careers. From both a present and future perspective, our success in such areas as family, finances, and physical and emotional health are more important than our success at work. All of us know people in law enforcement who will not retire because they have no families, hobbies, or any semblance of a personal life. Many of these individuals also seem to have a high probability of not living long after retirement or of going through problems such as alcohol abuse or other destructive behaviors.

If managing our personal lives is so important, why do most of us fail? Many of the reasons we fail as leaders in the workplace apply to personal issues as well. For example, individuals who are ineffective at home are often self-deceived and fail to discipline themselves. I believe, however, that we are often *more* prone to fail at home and in personal issues than in our careers because of additional factors that are not prevalent in the workplace.

First, accountability is critical to practicing effective skills at work. If other people or evaluation systems hold us accountable for not being conscientious in our duties, we will tend to discipline ourselves to do what we need to do, even when we don't feel like it. Though accountability structures in law enforcement agencies are often weak, in most of our personal lives, they are virtually nonexistent. If we fail to show up at work on time, someone is likely to confront us. If we consistently fail to be involved with our spouse and children, however, there is usually little or no system to show us that this is clearly unacceptable or to confront us. We may experience some discomfort about not doing what we should, but we can ignore these feelings if we choose. As a result, we are often much more undisciplined in the way we carry out our responsibilities outside the workplace.

Related to the issue of accountability is how we use our time. At work, time is generally not our own. We have fixed and designated amounts of time to accomplish projects, do evaluations, and perform tasks that have been given to us by others. When we get off work, however, we are generally free to use the time in whatever manner we wish. We can either use our time wisely or completely waste it. With that amount of freedom, we often tend to become undisciplined and inconsistent about scheduling time to work out, allocating time with our family or friends, or participating in a hobby.

Other factors that may contribute to failure in our personal lives are emotional and physical fatigue. Our physical and emotional energies are naturally focused on the workplace, especially in a profession where we have to engage and pay attention. As Gilmartin discusses in *Emotional Survival for Law Enforcement*, when we leave the workplace, our bodies (and our minds) will often go into neutral because of fatigue, both physical and emotional. We are generally tired when we get home, and it becomes routine and natural to feel that it is unimportant to talk with our spouse, help our children with their studies, or go to the gym for a workout. Our personal lives tend to get the leftovers of our energy reserves. As a result, we often fail to respond effectively to the tasks we know we should do.

It should therefore not be surprising that most of us who do a decent job at the workplace are often miserable failures in our personal lives. For that reason, this chapter has been the most problematic for me to write, because I have often been unsuccessful in implementing the strategies of this chapter consistently. I would never have classified myself as the most effective leader at work, but compared to my personal life, my work life was a resounding success. I have often not been an attentive father or husband, and most of my life I have been overweight and out of shape. If I had performed my work duties like I have handled my personal life, I would have been classified as a problem employee!

> *Most of us who do a decent job at the workplace are often miserable failures in our personal lives.*

The only way that I was able to complete this chapter was to do so knowing that these principles do in fact work, even if I have not consistently mastered them in my own life. How I know they work is based on two experiences. First, I have spent time with others who have been successful in their personal lives, and their behaviors were consistent with many of the skills discussed earlier that will apply to our personal lives in this chapter. I have been blessed to know many individuals who display leadership in their families and other aspects of their personal lives. Their ability to be successful in these areas was always related to their skills.

Second, I have had sporadic and brief periods of my life when I practiced these principles and was more successful as a result. During those times, I saw glimpses of how acting on the principles increased my effectiveness as a father and a husband, helped me better manage my finances, and improved my physical and emotional wellness. The bottom line is that we can be successful in our personal lives if we are willing to practice the same types of skills that make individuals successful as leaders in the law enforcement agency.

> *The secret of a leader lies in the tests he has faced over the whole course of his life and the habit of action he develops in meeting those tests.*
>
> —Gail Sheehy

Physical Fitness

I am purposely beginning this discussion with physical fitness because of its impact on other areas of our personal lives. Almost everything we do to live full and successful lives requires energy, and our level of physical fitness is critical to our ability to engage and handle various other facets of our lives. Two thirds of Americans are overweight, so most of us obviously do not handle this area of our lives very well.

Fitness is particularly important for those in law enforcement because policing is one of the few professions in which an acceptable level of fitness is required. Unfortunately, if you observe law enforcement personnel around the country, as I do regularly, you quickly see that they are as overweight and out of shape on average as other Americans who have no such occupational requirement.

Many excellent books on exercise and on diet are available, so I won't talk about particular programs or strategies here, but obviously most us are not getting in shape despite the wealth of information on how to do it. As with leadership and management, for which copious amounts of literature are also available, becoming fit is likely a matter of discipline, and many principles, particularly those of self-management (see page 62), apply to increasing and maintaining our physical wellness.

If you know any people who seem to keep on top of their fitness, you know that they schedule a specific time to work out regularly and rarely deviate—even if they don't feel like it at times. As with leadership techniques, if you don't schedule an activity, you probably won't do it. Most people I know who do well in this area schedule an hour per day about five times per week and are faithful to follow through on not missing most of these appointments to take care of themselves. Another leadership-related principle that they use is peer support and accountability; working out with others strongly reinforces their ability to exercise consistently. The final characteristic of individuals who do well in this area is their understanding of delayed gratification—they don't do it because they want to but because they know it is the right thing to do. Besides, they feel a sense of accomplishment after they discipline themselves to follow through—this technique is also a critical skill of a leader (see page 58).

Emotional Fitness

Much of our fatigue is not just physical, but emotional. Dealing with problem employees, bad management decisions, and irate citizens can make us feel like we have just played two back-to-back professional football games. Gilmartin's book *Emotional Survival for Law Enforcement* and other sources do an excellent job of examining this emotional aspect of our profession (see, for example, the Suggested Reading on page 151). Much of this literature recommends common techniques for managing stress and emotional fatigue that relate to some of the leadership strategies in this book.

Two of the best methods of handling stress are *exercise* and *hobbies*. Besides the physical benefits we gain from exercise, it is considered one of the most positive means to relieve stress. Another strategy, though less publicized, is to have a hobby. Most law enforcement personnel who handle the stress of the job well will often cite their hobbies as a means of coping with the frustrations of their work. They enjoy their off-duty hours because they can spend them on pleasurable activities, whether riding a motorcycle, building cabinets, or camping.

Hobbies give us a sense of control and satisfaction that is not available at work. So much of what happens in law enforcement and within the agency is out of our direct control. Hobbies provide us with a sense of accomplishment not found in the job and give us something to do constructively with our time when we are not at work. Hobbies, like exercise, usually require disciplining ourselves to schedule the activity or having others participate with us. I have found that many of the

> *Hobbies give us a sense of control and satisfaction that is not available at work. So much of what happens in law enforcement and within the agency is out of our direct control.*

most conscientious people at the workplace often do not use their organizational skills and discipline when they come home. Many will find that, as a result of this lack of discipline in their off time, they are bored and frustrated when they are on vacation or when they retire.

Not Bringing the Skills Home

My father enjoyed considerable success at work but failed to use the same skills at home. People who worked with my father commented on his faithfulness to follow through on requests and his discipline to do an exemplary job in everything he did. He always had a notebook of some type that he carried at work to remind him to do certain tasks. He seemed, however, to forget these skills completely when he came home, and he never followed through on his good intentions. He loved to fish but never scheduled time to do it. He was often frustrated and bored when he was home or on vacation. When he retired after forty-three years of service, his retirement was a disaster. Without his job to provide some sense of accomplishment, and with a long-established pattern at home of not following through or disciplining himself to do what he enjoyed, he began drinking heavily and was often frustrated and angry. He had not brought the skills home with him that had made him effective at work, and this failure made his last years a sad testimony of the importance of skills in all aspects of one's life.

Another strategy for dealing with stress is to spend regular time with our friends. As social creatures, we benefit from being around people with whom we have close relationships. Friends often take us more honestly than others do— they know us well enough to hold us accountable but will be forgiving of mistakes and outbursts. Friends add to us emotionally and are excellent candidates for helping us with exercise and hobbies. Many of us have several close friends, but unfortunately, we never seem to spend time with them. In our busy work and family schedules, we fail to schedule specific times with these important sources of emotional health. When we have a chance meeting with them, we enjoy the encounter but always end the time with a "we need to get together sometime" statement. We should learn instead to schedule a specific time to get together. If we do not, "sometime" will never seem to happen.

Improving Physical and Emotional Health

Why not get started by scheduling at least one health-related activity next week, such as exercise, a hobby, or spending time with friends or family? You might be able to schedule an activity that accomplishes two or more of those suggestions. For example, you might schedule an evening with family and friends to go bowling or to go walking at a nearby park.

Don't get frustrated if finding a time is difficult to do or if others are not enthusiastic. Start small and understand that if life is a skill and you have not done these things in a while, you will need to practice these behaviors to regain your ability to succeed in these areas. If you decide to exercise, start slow and be patient in your progress. Before attempting an exercise program, you might check with your doctor, who can provide advice and information to help you.

Besides developing positive off-duty habits like exercise, hobbies, and spending time with our friends, we need to avoid certain behaviors that increase our stress or cause us not to deal with problems that may be causing our stress. These often damaging escape behaviors include watching too much television, overeating, and working a part-time job. A part-time job may be a

Besides developing positive off-duty habits like exercise, hobbies, and spending time with our friends, we need to avoid certain behaviors that increase our stress or cause us not to deal with problems that may be causing our stress.

symptom of another escape behavior—spending more than we make. These behaviors often rob us of developing relationships with our family and friends or being involved in exercise or hobbies. Under the pretense of winding down, we can create a pattern of not developing skills in our personal lives or in handling stress, which in turn can lead us to blame our jobs for lack of fulfillment at home.

My Job Has Screwed Me Over with My Family

During a training program that I was doing, I had just mentioned that the job can be stressful and affect our families. A sergeant attending the class came up to me at the break and told me "the job has screwed me over with my family." He went on to elaborate that he usually worked from 8 A.M. until 7 P.M., and that his wife and children had little if anything to do with him and resented him. He blamed this alienation from his family completely on his long work hours. I asked him what time his family went to bed. He appeared puzzled and responded that it was usually around 10:30 or 11:00 P.M. I then asked him what he did between the time he got home and their bedtime, which according to my calculations was at least three hours. He looked flustered and responded that he needed time to unwind and would usually watch television. I asked him why he thought it was the police department's fault that he did not have a good relationship with his family when he spent the three hours a day he was home watching television—plenty of potential quality time with his spouse and each one of his children. He agreed that he had not looked at it that way until now.

Other addictive and escape behaviors can be more serious. Law enforcement personnel and managers sometimes engage in compulsive gambling or in alcohol and drug abuse to handle the stress in their lives. These dangerous behaviors usually result in serious outcomes such as demotion, termination, and even criminal prosecution. All of us have known of personnel who destroyed their careers and lives through addictive behaviors that began as an occasional drink or a wager on a game. Not handling stress through legitimate avenues such as exercise and hobbies may make us susceptible to more destructive behaviors. Even seemingly harmless habits like watching pornography can lead to problems at work or at home.

Family Relationships

This area of our personal lives may be the most important to our long-term emotional health and success. Law enforcement personnel's lack of success in marriage and relationships is well known, and I will not belabor the bad news or try to make anyone feel guilty for past failures. Instead, let's focus on how we can turn our feelings for our family into actual behaviors. Of course, the same principle you've encountered throughout this book applies here as well—good intentions must be acted upon. Most of us love our spouses and children but fail to follow through, just as ineffective managers fail to act on what they know they should do for employees. With this in mind, let's look at some specific applications of leadership skills to family issues.

> *Most of us love our spouses and children but fail to follow through, just as ineffective managers fail to act on what they know they should do for employees.*

Many of us did not have good modeling in our own families, and this skill deficit will usually affect us when we have our own families. Many of the strategies in chapters 5 through 7 can also be applied to becoming skilled in relationships. Specifically, we need to *discipline ourselves* to *learn the skills* we may have not seen in our own upbringing. We must *practice communication, sometimes writing out our positive thoughts* to our loved ones if we are not skilled at speaking them. Do not be afraid to ask others who seem competent in this area to mentor you and give you specific suggestions on how to be a better parent and spouse. *Having others hold you accountable* will also help you follow through on this skills development as you are learning.

Once you know what to do, don't forget the critical skills of *writing down and scheduling time to follow through* on the knowledge you have and on your good intentions. MBWA works in the family just as it works in the law enforcement agency, but if you don't schedule it, you will not follow through. Gilmartin's suggestion to schedule specific time and activities with our children every week is a practical application of this leadership skill. Learning to write down positive behaviors and activities to do with our family will always make us more faithful in our performance of them.

Scheduling Personal Time with Family Members

My wife suggested when our children were small that I allocate a weekly time to spend with each child. They each usually chose the type of activity, and I generally insisted that it did not include any of their friends. They normally chose activities such as going to the playground, wrestling with me, or playing some type of game. They were seemingly impressed that they had me to themselves and have remembered many of these "dates," even though they now have children of their own!

The listening and attending behaviors of proactive communication not only help us win the commitment of our subordinates at work; both are powerful communication strategies that work with the family. Seeking regular communication opportunities and then paying attention when these opportunities present themselves are critical to building relationships within our families. *Using good nonverbal communication* with our family members is an important skill to practice at home. Stopping what we are doing and fully attending to the person who is talking with us is a skill we all should learn and practice. Don't be surprised, however, if this is awkward for you to do, or if it is not accepted as genuine if you have never done it

> Commitment leads to action. Action brings your dream closer.
> —**Marcia Wieder**

before. Regardless of our skill level or the reception it receives, however, good nonverbal communication must be practiced to be mastered.

As with leadership, the most critical skill in improving our family relationships is *learning to discipline ourselves.* Doing the right thing even when we don't feel like it is always the narrow and less-traveled road of a leader—and of an effective parent and spouse. Going shopping with our spouse when we don't like shopping or throwing the ball to a small child when we want to watch television is the essence of leadership. Battling ourselves every day is the only way we will ever become one of the few who are effective at work and at home.

What Is He Guilty Of?

I was doing a presentation in front of several hundred female employees who were attending a conference in Texas for support staff in criminal justice agencies. When discussing the role of nonverbal communication, I did a role-play, pretending to be a husband intently watching his favorite television show when his wife came in and asked a question. I asked the participants what would happen if the husband turned off the television, turned toward the wife, leaned forward, and then asked, "What is it, darling?" The laughter was a continuous uproar, and I could not regain any sense of control of the audience for a minute or two. One woman jumped up and yelled from the back of the room, "He is obviously having an affair!" When I laughingly asked her why she thought that was the case, she responded, "He never pays attention unless he is guilty of something! He has a girlfriend, or he bought another gun and feels guilty about it!"

This chapter illustrates how the skills that make us effective as leaders in the workplace are identical to those necessary to living a full and rewarding life with our family and friends. Having the discipline to listen actively to a spouse's concerns about the budget or to confront a teenage daughter calmly and consistently requires the skills discussed in chapters 3 through 7. From the perspectives of time and long-term success, practicing these skills at home may be more important than practicing them at work.

Someone once told me that you really don't know if you have succeeded or failed in life until the end of the race. All of us know people who cannot enjoy the latter years of life because they never took the time to invest in relationships, develop hobbies, or take care of their physical health. Many Americans finish their lives discouraged, feeling that they wasted the time they were given. Though many seniors in this country have adequate financial resources, they often have poor or strained relationships with their families and are in poor health because of lack of exercise or other factors (like smoking cigarettes) that they chose to ignore. We now have the greatest life expectancy of any generation in history, but for what end?

> *We now have the greatest life expectancy of any generation in history, but for what end?*

All of us have also met older people who did *not* choose to neglect their personal lives. I was at a conference recently where I met an older man who had his wife of fifty-plus years with him, and it was obvious that they still enjoyed each other's company. He was thin but fit and told me of his plans to travel to Africa to hunt on foot in the rain forests of Cameroon. I could not help but note his sharp mind and enthusiasm for life—and he had just celebrated his eightieth birthday!

By our choices every day, we decide which of these types of lives we will ultimately have. If we are not willing to discipline ourselves to practice the skills of self-mastery, communication, and other aspects of leadership in our personal

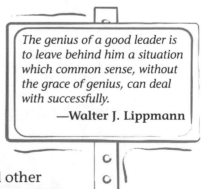

> *The genius of a good leader is to leave behind him a situation which common sense, without the grace of genius, can deal with successfully.*
> —**Walter J. Lippmann**

lives, we will finish the race in a mediocre and disappointing manner.

I can't think of a worse way to end life—to know that we failed to skillfully take advantage of the opportunities that we had during our lives. Unfortunately, most will choose that path. There is a better way, however, if we choose to be abnormal. At the end of the road less traveled are the winners of the race.

What It Really Takes to Lead

The Quest for Self-Mastery

Communication and Engagement Skills

Encouragement and Accountability Skills

Holistic Leadership

This final chapter summarizes the key points and conclusions we can draw about being effective as leaders in the law enforcement organization. Before doing that, however, I must again emphasize that these skills are critical because most of us are failing to do them in a consistent manner. The theme throughout chapter 4 is that most law enforcement managers are failing to be effective leaders. Only a handful of law enforcement managers and executives have ever disagreed with me on this statement. As I have stated before, most of these ineffective managers are wonderful people—they just fail to follow the road less traveled of the leader. Most of us fail ultimately because leadership is contrary to human nature and rare in the law enforcement culture—it is not going to be modeled or encouraged by our peers, who are also ineffective. Leadership in law enforcement is hard to do, and obviously most of us are not willing to pay the price.

Someone mentioned recently to me that most law enforcement agencies do fairly well in carrying out their operational duties despite most managers being ineffective. He believes that this is true because of the dedication of the personnel that we have—they do their job despite ineffective and evil managers. He believes that law enforcement personnel learn to work around poor managers and get the job done anyway. Though his statements made me feel proud of the dedication of our sworn and civilian personnel, I was also saddened by the idea of people having to do their jobs despite a lack of leadership. Don't these men and women deserve better? Let's review how we can turn this around.

The Quest for Self-Mastery

I think the foundation of being effective (or ineffective) as a leader is how we view ourselves. Leaders assume that leadership is difficult, so they practice self-mastery, obedience, and discipline as their highest forms of motivation. They do not concentrate on what managers around them are doing or not doing but focus on their own obedience to the principles of leadership. Leaders enjoy making themselves do what needs to be done, and they do it despite criticism or lack of approval. In a sense, they stand before an audience of one, seeking discipline and obedience so that they can face themselves at the end of the day. They also understand that this fight for self-control and walking the talk is a daily battle, and one that they will have to struggle with for the rest of their lives. As a result of these struggles and occasional failures, leaders never take themselves too seriously. Being self-aware, they know they have nothing to be egotistical about.

> *Whether a man is burdened by power or enjoys power; whether he is trapped by responsibility or made free by it; whether he is moved by other people and outer forces or moves them—this is the essence of leadership.*
>
> **—Theodore H. White**

Leaders have the same positive thoughts and belief systems as many of their ineffective counterparts, but they understand that the road to hell is paved with good intentions. As a result, they don't trust these thoughts unless there is some type of structure to turn them into actions. To do this,

leaders force themselves to write things down and to schedule specific times each week to follow through on their good
intentions. They understand that leadership by example is
ultimately the only way to be a leader.

Communication and Engagement Skills

Leaders pursue communication opportunities with others.
They invade the lives of others to know them, and they
become known to the men and women they supervise. They
refuse to sit behind their desks and
assume that anyone who needs to
talk to them will come to their
office. To put this philosophy into
operation, leaders schedule designated times each week to spend
talking individually and corporately with personnel. They are also keenly aware of spon-

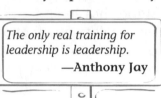

*The only real training for
leadership is leadership.*

—**Anthony Jay**

taneous encounters during the week when they have an
opportunity to communicate with those they meet in eleva-
tors, at training classes, or in the break room. Most important, they pay attention nonverbally and verbally to
personnel when these opportunities present themselves.
They understand that these encounters, both planned and
spontaneous, are critical moments to build commitment
and trust among individuals.

Encouragement and Accountability Skills

Leaders understand that they must reinforce their words
with both encouragement and accountability. They know
that their good thoughts are worthless and
that appreciation of exemplary
work and behavior is meaningless without spoken, written, and
tangible forms of encouragement. They also understand that
encouragement is not effective
unless they have the courage to confront
those exhibiting marginal and problem

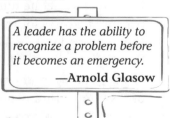

*A leader has the ability to
recognize a problem before
it becomes an emergency.*

—**Arnold Glasow**

behavior as well. Leaders care enough about the offending person, the affected people, and the professionalism of law enforcement not to let improper behavior go unchallenged. They are gracious about honest mistakes but aggressive toward unkind and evil behavior.

Holistic Leadership

Leaders also apply self-mastery, communication, and motivational skills to their lives outside of work. They understand that to engage life fully, they must keep themselves physically and emotionally fit for the long haul. They use discipline to engage their family and friends, even when they are tired. They proactively seek communication opportunities in their relationships, and turn off the television if someone needs to talk or get help with a science project. As a result, they enjoy their days off and their vacations and have the ability to enjoy their retirement because of the relationships and skills they have developed over the years.

A Man Who Took the Narrow Road

One of the great role models I have had in my life is my father-in-law. He is ninety years of age and was successful in his career as a federal manager, as a husband of sixty-three years, and as a father of six children. He has always practiced many of the skills of effective leadership described throughout this book. He has always paid attention and has disciplined himself to put others ahead of his own needs. He has always been a positive communicator and is one of the most encouraging human beings that I have known. Yet he has always held people accountable because he cares for them, and he would aggressively confront evil and unkind behavior, even if it was committed by one of his own children. He balanced his career and his family, and when they conflicted, he always opted in favor of his family. He still enjoys an occasional game of golf, and until several years ago, he played on a softball team as the senior member in a league where the minimum age was seventy!

As I spend time with him and observe his still sharp wit and sense of humor, I cannot help but think that he is truly an abnormal person. He chose to be a leader at work and at home, and learned and practiced the skills of managing himself, communication, motivation and accountability, and managing his personal life. As a result, he has completed his life as a success. Dozens of people enjoy spending time with him and are committed to his well-being, regardless of the cost. He is always surrounded by others, because he always invested in others.

Most of us will not choose his way. We will choose to do what we feel like doing, deny our weaknesses, and fail to follow through on our good intentions. We will choose career over family, and then have nothing to come home to when we retire. We will not be bad people, just normal, mediocre ones. We will choose to live our last days embittered about how our job screwed us and perplexed that no one ever comes to see us. Our family members will visit us, but out of obligation, not commitment and devotion. All because we did not discipline ourselves to be different, but took the path of least resistance—where most people spend their lives.

Life basically comes down to two roads. One road is very narrow, and only a few people will have the discipline or the skills to travel it. The rest of us will likely choose the wide and easy road—and we will not be leaders. We have failed to produce leaders in our law enforcement agencies because we have assumed leadership is easy to do. As we have seen by the failure rate, both at work and at home, of managers in our departments, leadership may be the hardest thing to do in human experience. Failure to believe that will always cause us to fail.

Much of what we have discussed throughout these chapters has no doubt seemed overwhelming. I have found that this sense of being overwhelmed is beneficial, however, if I use it as a motivation to change. Seeing ourselves as having failed can always be the beginning of modifying our behavior and beginning to discipline ourselves to change. If you have now felt this need to improve, remember that change is a process that takes time. As a friend of mine reminded me, you cannot wake up some morning and decide to run a marathon. So is the process of personal change and growth. Identify two or three keys areas and work on them, but ask someone to help you. Have this person hold you accountable to a realistic time line, but celebrate even small successes. You do not have to be flawless or fast in your journey—just moving ahead at a slow and sporadic pace is better than what most people are doing. Self-mastery is a slow and often painful process—but it is the only way to win the race.

> *He who chooses the beginning of a road chooses the place it leads to. It is the means that determine the end.*
>
> **—Harry Emerson Fosdick**

I turned fifty-five in 2005 and have discussed with many of my fellow boomers how time is passing so quickly. I began my career in law enforcement in 1972 and have taught classes to many first-line supervisors who had not been born when I became a police officer! Perhaps this book is an attempt to pass on to this next generation of law enforcement managers my thoughts on why my generation failed to produce many leaders for the law enforcement culture. Life is too short to spend our careers self-deceived, undisciplined, and mediocre. As American society becomes more unskilled and uncertain, the demands on the American law enforcement culture will only increase. We need leaders who are abnormal and different from most. This was the purpose of this book, and I pray that it will help you in your journey.

Leadership Effectiveness Evaluation

Please rate your manager or supervisor from 0 to 10 on each of the following criteria.

1. Integrity and honor: moral and legal standards; truth-fulness operationally and with personnel

   0 = consistently lies; corrupt; little or no integrity; untrust-worthy
   5 = inconsistent moral and ethical standards; tells you what you want to hear
   10 = high moral standards; consistently honest with employees

Score: _____

Comments: _____

_____

_____

2. Communication: verbal and nonverbal interaction with personnel; listening skills

   0 = talks only when angry; demeaning interaction; won't listen; no contact with employees
   5 = sporadic contact with employees; some listening
   10 = consistent ongoing contact with all employees; always willing to listen

Score: _____

Comments: _____

_____

_____

3. Accountability: use of rewards and discipline; contact regarding good, marginal, and bad behavior

   0 = focuses only on discipline or totally ignores bad or marginal behavior
   5 = inconsistent use of rewards and discipline; favoritism
   10 = consistent, ongoing feedback on good and bad behavior of all employees

Score: _____

Comments: _____

_____

_____

_____

4. Mentorship: concern for employee welfare and professional development

   0 = does not care for employees professionally or personally; self-centered
   5 = sporadically concerned for employees; occasional favoritism
   10 = wants all employees to succeed; teaches others; cares for all employees

Score: _____

Comments: _____

_____

_____

_____

5. Temperament and attitude: emotional stability; anger management; positive attitude

0 = always negative about job and people
5 = up and down emotionally; inconsistent and unpredictable
10 = calm and predictable; consistently positive about people and mission

Score: _____
Comments: _____

_____

_____

_____

6. Professionalism: operational skills; commitment to learning and training

0 = a "dinosaur"; little or no operational expertise; unskilled
5 = limited or narrow operational skills; somewhat outdated; "desk jockey"
10 = competent professional; ongoing growth in job and experience

Score: _____
Comments: _____

_____

_____

_____

_____

7. Fairness: equitable treatment of employees in all issues

  0 = shows blatant favoritism; inconsistent in rewards and
      discipline
  5 = shows some favoritism; occasionally partial in
      rewards and discipline
10 = treats all employees fairly; does not show favoritism
      in rewards or discipline

Score: _____

Comments: _____

_____

_____

_____

_____

Suggested Reading

The Arbinger Institute. *Leadership and Self-Deception: Getting Out of the Box.* San Francisco: Berrett-Koehler Publishers, 2002.

Cohen, William A. *The Stuff of Heroes: The Eight Universal Laws of Leadership.* Marietta, Ga.: Longstreet, 1998.

Gilmartin, Kevin M. *Emotional Survival for Law Enforcement: A Guide for Officers and Their Families.* Tucson, Ariz.: E-S Press, 2002.

Maxwell, John C. *The 21 Irrefutable Laws of Leadership: Follow Them and People Will Follow You.* Nashville, Tenn.: Thomas Nelson Publishers, 1998.

Phillips, Donald T. *Lincoln on Leadership: Executive Strategies for Tough Times.* New York: Warner Books, 1992.

Polansky, Brian J. *Communication Excellence: Change Your Words, Change Your World.* Little Rock, Ark.: Arrow Ridge Publishing, 2005.

Sampson, Stephen J., John D. Blakeman, and Robert R. Carkhuff. *Social Intelligence Skills for Law Enforcement Supervisors/Managers.* Amherst, Mass.: HRD Press, 2006.

Smith, Perry M. *Rules and Tools for Leaders: A Down-to-Earth Guide to Effective Managing.* New York: Perigee, 2002.